NICARAGUA
A Decade of Revolution

The text of this book was composed in Times Roman (Adobe Systems, Inc.)
on an Apple Macintosh IIcx computer using Aldus PageMaker™ 3.02
Manufactured by Dai Nippon Printing Company, Ltd.
Book design by Stephanie Sherman, Lou Dematteis
Cover design by Fuenteovejuna

First Edition

ISBN 0-393-02965-4
ISBN 0-393-30739-5 (pbk)

W. W. Norton & Company, Inc., 500 Fifth Avenue, New York, N.Y. 10110

W.W. Norton & Company, Inc., 10 Coptic Street, London, England WC1A 1PU

1 2 3 4 5 6 7 8 9 0

NICARAGUA
A Decade of Revolution

Edited by Lou Dematteis with Chris Vail

Introduction by Eduardo Galeano
Text by Anthony Jenkins

W.W. Norton New York / London

This book is dedicated to all those Nicaraguans
who gave their lives during the decade of revolution.

These photographs, beautiful and terrible, pay homage to a reality both beautiful and terrible.

*Perhaps these texts of mine can serve as a doorway, so that the reader may
penetrate that reality. They are three steps in a process that is still alive, astounding and
powerful, beyond the electoral reversal suffered by the Sandinistas.*

—Eduardo Galeano

FIRST DAY IN NICARAGUA
1980

I

To get to Nicaragua, please stop by the Miami airport. I believe there is no better way to get to a barefoot revolution. Please remain a few hours at the Miami airport and take a peek at the noisy world of the Latin millionaires and the middle class that wishes it could do what it cannot but acts as if it could. This is a sanctuary for dictators and their bullies, a never-ending carnival of consumerism and bad taste, center of the universal culture of plastic and tin and machines that manufacture emotions. Sit down and look around you, it's worth it. See the men who are or have been the owners of other men, kneeling down in front of goods. The store windows are altars. Things buy people. And he who is not for sale is for hire.

Passing through the Miami airport, I can see the campaign commercials on a TV screen. Carter erects a wall in the face of the overwhelming Reagan offensive: a wall, a confident smile, a close-up, color, teeth. "We are still," he assures us, "the most powerful on Earth."

II

The Managua airport is now called Augusto César Sandino airport. The road to the city is paved with bricks. I had never seen a road like this. I remark that it seems as if it's from colonial times. Yes, says Lisandro Chávez Alfaro. The paving stones are from colonial times—Somoza's. The dictator made these bricks and sold them to the State. A good business that turned against him: with these stones the people erected the barricades.

Few cars. Their license plates say "Nicaragua Libre." Alongside the road, Sandinista flags and billboards for Fanta and Citizen and posters of the revolution. On an Agrarian Reform banner, the words of a peasant agitator tortured and murdered by Somoza: "We are not birds that live in the air, nor fish that live in the sea. We are men who live from the land." Ruins made by bombs. Emergency housing, erected in the middle of vast green spaces: wooden shacks with tin roofs. From the plane I had seen the shining tin roofs and had imagined the poor people frying under the burning sun.

We are still in the middle of the countryside when our friends say: "Here we are."

"Where?"

"In Managua."

We are in Managua. After the earthquake and the war, Managua is this enormous ruin or campsite in the midst of all this green. In 1972, the earth shook like an angry stallion. It undulated and trembled and destroyed the city. The Marines flew from Panama to protect Somoza, the same Marines that 35 years before had installed his father on the throne. Somoza took charge of the situation. He created a demolition company and bought the biggest construction company. The dictator had a good eye for business. The Chief of State signed contracts with himself. He called Nicaragua "my farm." His fatherland was his patrimony. Help came from all over the world to increase his fortune. "I am left of center," he used to say in those days. The earthquake killed 12,000 people, according to the official figures. Three hundred thousand were left homeless.

Then came the war. The revolution cost more lives than the oscillations of the earth, and now, in the center of Managua, children play with what is left of the tanks. In the cathedral's bell tower, an empty and slanted shell, the clock still marks the time of the catastrophe, a little past 12:30, while the front sports an immense figure of Sandino.

III

The dictator was crazy about bathrooms and mirrors. He had 16 bathrooms in the house he was occupying before taking refuge in the bunker. One of those bathrooms is now the office of the Vice Minister of Culture. The Minister's office has two bathrooms. The faucets in the hand basin are bronze eagles. On the desk of the Minister, poet Ernesto Cardenal, lies the tip of the tail of the senior Somoza's bronze horse. Many years before the revolution, the poet had prophesied that some day the people would bring down that statue.

Also at the Ministry of Culture, in the garden of Somoza's house, nature anticipated history. One morning the chilamate, a gigantic tree that reigned over the garden giving an enormous shadow, turned up on its side. It had uprooted itself and was lying there in the patio, with its roots in the air, while Enrique, the guacamayo, screeched in his cage. That day Somoza fell under a hail of bullets in Asunción, Paraguay.

"Who killed him?" the journalists asked Tomás Borge, the Minister of the Interior and founder of the Sandinista Front.

"Fuenteovejuna," answered Tomás Borge.*

IV

It is not that house, but the bunker that best symbolizes the system. It was in the bunker that Somoza lived his last days in Nicaragua. The garage is next to the bedroom and the bathrooms have telephones. Among plastic plants and countless mirrors the dictator read *The Ministry of Goodness* by Elena G. White, the latest American best-sellers, and *Management Information Systems Handbook*. Outside, the world was burning, but the bunker was a sound-proof steel structure, an enormous velvet-lined coffin where neither the screams nor the bullets nor the rain could be heard. "We must stimulate tourism," ordered the dictator in the midst of the war.

V

A war of sticks and stones and slings and home-made bombs. "Look," they tell me in Estelí, in León, in Masaya, "the houses have smallpox, because of the shooting." There's a prize for anyone who can find a wall that has not been bitten by the bullets; and among the standing walls, vast holes have been left by the rockets and the bombs.

In the Monimbo quarter in Masaya, which rose and fought to the end, many died. Two months after the victory, the survivors came out of the ruins to celebrate the "Toro Venado" festivities. Gaiety exploded as the rebellion had exploded. The "Devil" directed traffic and among the drinking and the laughter, the floats, improvised with sugar cane, palms and whatever else there was filed by. One of the floats displayed the making of home-made bombs in a corn grinding stone. "Death is no more than a moment of annoyance," Sandino had said, "and it's not worth taking seriously."

Augusto César Sandino had been murdered by the senior Somoza, the first of the dynasty, 45 years before. The dictatorship outlawed Sandino's name and image. The hero of the national resistance and the voice of the poor, had escaped from the cemetery.

VI

After plunder, the earthquake, and the war, the task is not easy. The Sandinistas have found a country in ruins: without schools or hospitals, no sewers or drinking water, sick with tuberculosis and malaria, and where one child in five dies.

"The first step was the dissolution of Somoza's National Guard," the novelist Sergio Ramírez, a member of the Government Junta, explains to me. "We didn't even leave the band behind." Then the nationalizations. For the first time the country took over its own basic resources and the profits these generated. "The mafia of thieves were not many. Perhaps 25,000, who are now in Miami. They lived as if they were in Miami, and they kept houses there because they knew one day they would end up there." Large land and forest holdings, Somoza's and his minions', went to the State, and so did a good portion of the industries. Foreign companies lost possesion of the gold and silver mines, the national savings, insurance, and foreign trade.

But the revolution is in the first day of Creation. "We are just beginning. There is still everything left to do," says Tomás Borge, and he half-closes his eyes, as if aiming: "We sell the cotton and buy the thread. We spend hard currency on oil though we have the energy of the rivers and the volcanoes. We need at least, to give a low estimate, 200,000 houses urgently. How many can we build? With luck, 35,000."

A revolution in poverty, in a poor country. The New Nicaragua press agency was born the day a group of journalists were out walking around the Managua market. Someone was trying to sell a "typewriter with a telephone" at the top of his lungs.

"How much?"

The journalists put the money together among themselves, the equivalent of $50.00, and took the telex with them.

VII

A young revolution. Most of them are under 30 years old, the commanders, the ministers, the vice ministers. The Sandinista guards are still boys.

Two soldiers talk in front of the door to one of the ministries; Sergio Ramírez has just announced that there is proof of foreign financing of a mutiny at Bluefields and of the armed bands. One of the soldiers asks, "And why don't we declare war on the United States?"

The other soldier responds, "You're crazy. They are something like 250 million."

"Oh. We can't, then."

"No. We can't."

"Ah."

And after a while, "And why can't we?"

"Can't you see we don't have anywhere to put that many prisoners?"

The country will be for everyone. The revolution already is. Proud of their land, the "Nicas" are beginning to walk on their own two feet. At León, in the midst of a landscape of ruins, where a burning smell still lingers in the air, a student tells me, "How lucky you are. I'd like so much to be from somewhere else so I could come here and learn about this country!"

Nicaragua is in a state of assembly. The people organize, argue and make decisions.

"Those who keep criticism to themselves," warns commander Daniel Ortega, "will be accomplices to the mistakes." And the Interior Minister himself, commander Tomás Borge, is the first to denounce the abuses and arbitrary actions committed by his men.

VIII

The peasant who has gone to find the priest is close to 90 years old. He tells him, "Father, I want to marry a fairy."

The old man asks the priest to baptize the fairy first, so she will become flesh and blood; the priest says that he cannot baptize the fairy unless she materializes.

"Tell her that unless she becomes a person, there's nothing I can do."

"And how can I? She's been with me for years but has never spoken to me."

"Explain to her that you have honest intentions."

"If you could just see her, Father. She is so beautiful."

Alejandro von Reichnitz, the Jesuit priest, is recounting his experiences in the literacy campaign in *Barricada*, the newspaper of the Sandinistas. He had been teaching reading and writing in an isolated town, cut off by the mountains and the rains that would fall for 10 days in a row, where those that reach it, do so on horseback. He saw pale children with pot bellies—"real walking zoos, which a collector of parasites would be proud to exhibit"— girls bald with scabies infestations, men and women like ghosts, and even a young girl who declared herself dead by obliterating herself in bed.

The literacy campaign struck like lightning. More than half of all Nicaraguans did not know how to read and write. In five months, the level of illiteracy was reduced to 13 per cent. Now the literacy campaign will be in other languages—Miskito and other Indian languages and in English, which is what the black population of the Caribbean coast speaks. Of the 13 percent who are still illiterate, none will remain so other than those who are so nearsighted they "can't see three on a donkey."

La revolución. Those were the two key words for the literacy campaign workers. They contain all the vowels.

IX

For the first time, Nicaragua begins the task of national unity. The literacy campaign permitted the country, to a great extent, to discover itself. From the fields, the jungles, and the mountains the young people returned to the cities. They brought back new knowledge, they learned much. They also brought intestinal parasites, malaria; and their skin turned into strainers by mosquitoes, fleas, and ticks. "I can understand the horror of some city people," writes Father von Reichnitz. "What I cannot understand is why they are horrified that their children spend a few months in these conditions, but not that 70 percent of Nicaraguans have lived like this all their lives." And he adds, "It's a shame that this country's Christianity did not stop such injustice from being committed for more than 400 years."

X

Eastern Nicaragua—the Caribbean coast or Atlantic Coast—has always lived apart from the rest of the country. This other world is now the most vulnerable zone. The people of the Atlantic Coast did not participate in the long struggle against Somoza; and in its jungles there are people who do not even know there were dictators with that name. At the end of September there was a mutiny in Bluefields against the Cuban teachers and doctors working in the region. Of the 1,000 teachers and 300 doctors sent by Cuba, the majority are working in the more inhospitable and inaccessible places. Many are in the Atlantic Coast. "Are you crazy?" answered Borge on TV. "Are you crazy? In this country where schools are a luxury and where we have a terrifying infant mortality, you think we are going to send away the Cuban teachers and doctors that have come to give everything without asking for anything?"

XI

If the English speaking coast is difficult, the Indian region is even more so. The Miskitos call all other Nicaraguans "Spaniards" and have a very ancient and legitimate fear and distrust of them.

On the Honduran frontier, along the Río Coco, the literacy campaign in the native languages has taken off. It rains in Waspam. It rains as in a García Márquez story. It always rains: it rains nine straight months every year. The rains have taken 24 bridges. They cannot be rebuilt until the brief dry season comes. Bridges are not the only thing lacking around here. Of every ten natives, nine do not know how to read and write. There are no hospitals, but there is more than enough sickness to go around. There are no roads, vehicles, or fuel for the vehicles. The bamboo houses with palm roofs do not have septic tanks or lightning rods. First task: dig septic tanks and install lighting rods; explain that water should be boiled before drinking it. First

stage: teach the Miskitos to read and write in their own language. The Indians debate their problems in their native language. When they can't understand a situation, they act it out. Actors tell this story: there is a motor boat navigating the river, because in a raft on or a canoe it takes 10 days to bring the bananas from some towns. Another mime successfully explains that many drank the money that was to go for planting beans; and a girl shows how the Indian women that go down river end up as whores.

Ernesto Cardenal speaks: "We are discovering our identity, made up of diverse cultures, like your culture. We are learning." He explains that the literacy workers will pick up myths, legends, traditions, and testimonies of recent times, dances and songs.

Unanimously, the assembly asks for a guitar for him.

XII

"We are here on loan now. It will be they themselves who will resolve their problems," one of the literacy coordinators says to me in Waspam. His name is Fabio and he is 23 years old, and he doesn't know his daughter, born 11 months ago.

"You haven't been back to Masaya for a whole year?"

He doesn't give me a speech.

"That's the way these things are," he says.

XIII

The same humility is true of Tomás Borge, although he has fought for 20 years and is old enough to be the father of all these youngsters who are changing the country. I have to bite myself to keep from congratulating him. He always remembers and applies a sentence by Carlos Fonseca Amador, another founder of the Sandinista Front killed by the dictatorship: "You must criticize looking straight in the eyes, and you must praise behind one's back."

An unexpected reader of Juan Carlos Onetti, Tomás Borge asks me about him. He tells me that no sooner had he been named Minister of the Interior that he looked in his own voluminous police files but was unable to find what he was looking for. He looked and looked, but could not find it. He was looking for a piece of paper. On that paper he had written something he no longer remembered and that he now wished to have. After an eternity of beatings and questions, the Somocista guards gave him a piece of paper to write down his confession. On that paper, Tomás Borge wrote a poem to his daughter, born only a short time before.

XIV

José Coronel Urtecho writes, "Not even what was, is as it used to be."

The primitive painters of Solentiname, who announced the coming of paradise, are now beginning to build it.

And the writer Gioconda Belli remembers what a nine year-old girl told her: "Me, in my veins, instead of blood, I have laughter."

---

*Fuenteovejuna is a fictional village in a 16th century novel of the same name set in 15th century Spain, by Lope de Vega Carpio. A rebel against King Ferdinand and Queen Isabella causes disruption in the town of Fuenteovejuna; the villagers unite to oppose and kill him. They make a pact among themselves to never reveal who murdered him, to reply, "Fuenteovejuna lo hizo" (Fuenteovejuna did it) when asked. The townspeople keep their agreement until Ferdinand finally pardons them all, and peace and harmony are restored to the village.

In Defense of Nicaragua
1986

The pitiless and ever-growing siege and blockade are not occurring because there is no democracy in Nicaragua, but so that there shall not be any. They are not occurring because a dictatorship exists in Nicaragua, but so that one may exist once again. They are not occurring because Nicaragua is a satellite, a sad pawn on the chessboard of the great powers, but so that it may become one again. They are not occurring because Nicaragua is furnishing arms to neighboring countries, but so it shall no longer be able to furnish its example: a dangerous, contagious example of national independence and popular participation. In order to annihilate Nicaragua, it is essential that it be degraded and isolated. The revolution's enemies oblige it to defend itself, then accuse it for having done so. They want Nicaragua to be nothing more than a barracks: a vast barracks of hungry people.

One of the Contra leaders defines Nicaragua as *the country of "there isn't any"*; and he is right about that. The revolution has more than enough dignity, creative enthusiasm, and all those things the Contra's millions couldn't buy, but it lacks machinery and spare parts, medicine, clothing, and all the basics of a daily diet: oil, rice, beans, corn. Everyone complains, and they do so out loud. The continuous economic restrictions are disheartening and lower the energy level. The war has made its way to the dinner table and into the remotest corner of every home. People start lining up at dawn, hoping to get rationed food. A whole sackful of bills are needed to buy just a handful of goods on the black market. Two days a week there is no water in Managua, the capital, one of the hottest cities in the world, condemned by its climate to an incessant thirst. Power outages are frequent Telephones, scarce as they are, don't work. When the number answering is the one dialed, it's considered a miracle.

There's no fertilizer, to cite another case. And when some is found, there are no small planes spread it. If somehow spare parts are improvised so that the broken-down planes can fly again, then the war makes it impossible to harvest the cotton from the fertilized lands. The war: the invaders blow up bridges, machine-gun farmers, set fire to crops, mine harbors, set up ambushes on the roads, they destroy schools and health centers. Pincers of the same tongs are the trade blockade by the United States, the offended power, and the financial barrier set up by many governments, international credit establishments and world banks that had poured money into the Somoza dynasty the moment the Marines placed it on the thrown a half a century ago.

One must also add—and it is no less important—the mistakes that the revolutionaries themselves have made. Inevitable and numerous are the errors of a colonial country as it sets about to change itself into a real nation and stand on its own two feet, starting to walk, stumbling along without any imperialist crutches. It is well known that underdevelopment implies a whole tradition of inefficiency, an inheritance of ignorance, a fatalistic acceptance of impotence as inevitable destiny. It is very difficult to get out of this trap. Not impossible; and day by day on the vast and tormented outskirts of the capitalist world, other nations are also accomplishing the task of being born, in spite of the veto imposed by their masters. Not impossible, I say, but very difficult.

The Daily Invasion

Are we on the eve of an invasion of Nicaragua? The warning bugles sound and resound, announcing the imminent military intervention of the United States. The world responds with words more than deeds. Solidarity is declared more than practiced. The rhetoric of these declarations barely conceals the growing indifference. We are not lying when we say that Nicaragua is not alone, but saying so is not enough. The promise of support *in case* an invasion occurs and denunciations against a *threatened* intervention can easily turn out to be decorous ways of shrugging one's shoulders at the daily sacrifice made by this people, so dignified and so abandoned, for it is no longer a matter of being on alert to possible invasion, a possible intervention: *Nicaragua is being invaded every single day*, every day it pays a horrible price in blood and in fire, while the bold-faced intervention of the United States, recently made official by a vote of the one hundred million dollars, is unbelievably shocking

The United States has given the order for asphyxiation. The military invasion, openly planned, financed, and directed by it, is coupled with a sentence of isolation, handed down against Nicaragua by nearly all the Western countries, and the state of siege to which the merchants and bankers have condemned it, in order to force its surrender through hunger.

The Imperial Strategy

Ever since it became more or less clear that the Sandinista revolution was serious and that it planned to break out of the straitjacket of neocolonialist capitalism, the system made up its mind to wipe it out. If wiping it out is not possible, since that would imply the extermination of the majority of the population, the system wants, at least, to deform it. Deforming the revolution would be, after all, a way of annihilating it: *deforming it to the point that no one can recognize himself within it*. If indeed it survives, let it survive mutilated, and mutilated in its essential parts.

Continuous aggression calls for defense, and defense in a war like this, a war of life or death, a war of homeland or nothing, leads to a progressive militarization of the whole society, and that militarization, in turn, acts objectively against areas of democratic plurality and popular creativity. Military structures, vertical and authoritarian by definition, do not get on well with doubt, much less with dissent. Discipline, necessary for efficiency, is in direct contradiction to the development of the critical consciousness which is necessary so that the revolution not become its own mummy. Furthermore, the concentration of resources in internal security and national defense, which devours 40 percent of the budget and absorbs half of what the country produces, paralyzes those formidable projects for the transformation of reality that the revolution had put into practice in health, education, energy, communications. . .

A bombardment of lies accompanies the military and economic assault. The four points of the compass are regaled once again with the ruthless story of yet another revolution that has betrayed its own aspirations. This propaganda wears the false face of disappointment. Relief for cynics, consolation for deserters, alibis for the greedy: let no one be bothered with the belief that change is a possible venture. May the peoples of the so-called Third World, victims and witnesses of outside decisions, not suffer from the delusion that they are protagonists; their revolutionary leaders have also denied them bread and are leading them by the nose. It is quite clear, the propaganda points out: anti-imperialist movements and social revolutions murder freedom in the name of justice, and from the heights of power they deny the democracy they had promised from down below. Poor countries are condemned, therefore; they can only emerge from one dictatorship to fall into another, they can only choose between one concentration camp and another. The Lie Machine repeats over and over again: well-intentioned people in the Third World don't lose their way through any fault of imperialist attack, but through Russian perfidy and the irresistible Stalinist temptation that inexorably leads all revolutions that have taken place, or are taking place in the world, to the Gulag.

"They Force Us to Die and to Kill"

Let no one be confused. The Nicaraguan people protest, and loudly, about the many things that are lacking, but they do not ignore all they have—the rights and aspirations that they have for the first time in their history, and they face bullets for them. They fight for the legitimate right to defend themselves, not as a profession, nor for money, nor for a desire for territory, nor a will to power.

Nicaragua allocates 40 percent of its budget to defense and police, but Nicaragua is at war with the leading world power. Uruguay, a respected democracy, spends the same percentage on its armed forces, much smaller than the swelling columns of militia and people's army in Nicaragua, and it should be noted that no foreign power is invading Uruguay or threatening it on its borders. The relative weight of the armed forces of a country cannot be evaluated except by the function of their aims. Weapons to keep watch over the people are one thing; arms in the hands of a people on watch are another.

"They force us to die and they force us to kill," Tomás Borge, founder of the Sandinista Front has explained. Armed resistance to aggression painfully reveals the collective dignity of a people *forced into violence from without*, and although it is quite true that the rules of war impose an inevitable verticalism, and in the trenches orders take the place of explanations, it is no less true that an armed people is a proof of democracy. The fact that there are 300,000 Nicaraguans, soldiers and militiamen, armed with rifles, some in exchange for a meager salary and the majority in exchange for nothing, shows that this bizarre Sandinista tyranny is not afraid to arm the people, who, according to the enemy, are anxious to overthrow it.

A thousand and one times they tell us that Nicaragua is to blame for the armed conflict in Central America. Under the pretext of defending itself, they tell us, Nicaragua attacks. Yet not a single serious piece of proof has been put forth to show that Nicaragua has been supplying guerrillas in El Salvador or Guatemala. Besieged on land, sea, and air, spied upon from ships, airplanes, and satellites controlled by high-technology instruments that can photograph a mosquito on the horizon, how is it possible for Nicaragua to send ammunition or combatants to countries that are not even on its borders? On the other hand, the United States has brazenly used the territory of Honduras as a training base and platform for the mercenary invaders, and it is a notorious fact that the Honduran military takes part in aggressive operations against Nicaragua. Cost Rica is also a sanctuary for the Contras, although with a cover-up that befits its quiet tradition—yes, but no; yes, but more or less; yes, but don't let anyone see. Honduras and Costa Rica, who accuse Nicaragua, are systematically violating the principle of nonintervention in the internal affairs of their set-upon neighbor.

There is no government in the Americas or in Europe, democracy or dictatorship, democraship or dictatorcy, that doesn't feel authorized to propose, discuss, and, perhaps, impose some *solution* for *the problem* of Nicaragua, which is the same as saying *the problem* of Central America. This gives the impression that when it took on the transformation of Nicaragua, the Sandinista revolution brought about an unpardonable cataclysm. One that challenges the powerful and violates the law of universal balance: if it weren't for Nicaragua, Central America would be enjoying peace and happiness, or at least would cease disturbing the good order of the world. *Calling* for change is permitted, proclaiming it to the sky may even become necessary, but *making* that change, transforming reality—this scandalizes the gods.

Everybody has been giving Nicaragua the Democracy test. President Reagan, for example, doesn't find the elections, which confirmed the present authorities in Nicaragua by a wide majority of votes, worthy of belief. Perhaps he harbors the hope that Nicaragua will return to truly free elections such as the ones organized by Brigadier General Frank Ross McCoy of the United States Army. On November 4, 1928, the North American military oversaw and approved electoral registrations, and set up and presided over all polling places. General McCoy, who had been designated by the President of the United States to take over as director of the Electoral Council of Nicaragua, took charge of the vote count. Curiously, on that occasion the candidate preferred by the United States emerged victorious.

It is both comic and an indignity that Reagan should be echoed by certain Latin American professional politicians, foisted upon us as experts on Nicaraguan democracy. As everyone knows, manipulation and fraud are the custom in Latin America. Even the fiercest dictatorships have learned to put on a show of periodic elections held under a state of siege, in order to put together parliaments where opposition legislators give that small, indispensable, decorative touch. With or without a dictatorship, in most Latin American countries the people vote but do not elect, and the ceremonies of official political life are projected, like the deceitful shadows of a magic lantern, against the background of an atrociously antidemocratic social reality.

Giving a Floor to Democracy

Honest opponents—and they do exist—would have to recognize, at least, that during these seven years the Sandinista revolution has done the possible and the impossible in *laying the bases of justice and sovereignty necessary for democracy to be something other than a castle in the air*, a pro forma tax paid to the reigning hypocrisy, a joke on people who have nothing and decide nothing.

Only the development of the revolutionary consciousness and the daily confirmation of national dignity in the face of an enemy opposing them with bullets can explain the unusual process of discussion of the text of the new constitution that has been taking place throughout this past period. Even in the midst of war and in spite of the notorious organizational difficulties, *a hundred thousand Nicaraguans have discussed the draft of a constitution set forth by the Sandinista Front and five other political parties*. The new constitution is not being cooked up behind the backs of the people. In 72 open local councils nationwide, the most diverse points of view have been aired, without it occurring to anyone that divergence might be mistaken for heresy or doubt for weakness, and 1,500 amendments to the draft have been proposed.

The councils have relied—and this must be stressed—on a very broad female participation. Machismo is still alive, but it's not alive and kicking; recently it's been seen with its tail between its legs, in rather poor shape, while little by little, day by day, women are losing the fear of voicing their opinions and fears of other things as well. Numerous and furious female voices have been raised in the councils against the legacy of the old laws and outdated codes: it is no longer so easy to treat women with impunity as beasts of burden or mental inferiors.

During the last years of the Somoza dictatorship, several women attained rightly deserved positions of leadership in the guerrilla struggle. At the present moment there are women in the Sandinista government at the highest levels of responsibility; few women in relation to the many who deserve to be there because of their merit and talents, but Nicaragua is, for example, one of the few countries in the world where a woman heads up the police force. Doris Tijerino, who had been tortured and raped by Somoza's police, is the national chief of police. For the first time in Nicaraguan history there is a woman in charge; and for the first time there is a police force that does not torture or rape.

NATIONAL INDEPENDENCE

Nicaragua is waging a war against decolonization. *The President of the United States and the Pope in Rome, who assume the right to put Nicaragua in the dock of the accused, ought to begin by seeking its forgiveness or keeping their mouths closed.* It was the American military invaders who created the first of the Somozas during the '20s, and in the '30s they placed him on the throne in order to perpetuate the colonialist occupation. Viceroy Somoza, founder of the dynasty that so humiliated Nicaragua, received perpetual decorations from the United States, and no less perpetual blessings from the Vatican, and in the end he was buried with the honors of a Prince of the Church.

It so happens that Nicaragua refuses to go on being a caricature of a country, and the war is punishment for its insolent challenge. Only in the light of that struggle for national liberation, only in the light of that defensive war can certain measures of the Sandinista government be understood. This is the case of the suspension of the newspaper *La Prensa*. One might ask what would have happened back in 1776, in the midst of the United States' war for independence. Could there have been the free publication of a propaganda organ of the British Empire in Boston or Philadelphia or any other city that had recently achieved its freedom? Could enemies of the patriotic cause have had full freedom of expression?

The North American politicians and journalists who head up the current campaign against Nicaragua are only spreading the same old poisons that other American politicians and journalists spread throughout the world in Sandino's time. In this way they are spreading a thick smoke screen over a process that in the end is seeking the right to breathe freely without asking the permission of the great powers. When Augusto César Sandino's crazy little army rose up against colonialist occupation, *The Washington Herald* and other North American newspapers called Sandino a *Bolshevik agent* and declared that he was acting on orders from Mexico and in the service of Soviet expansion in Central America. Mexico was the Cuba of the time: President Calles had imposed intolerable taxes on American oil enterprises, and so the manipulators of public opinion pointed to him as an agent of Moscow and chose him to be the scapegoat of the Central American crisis of the time. Some organs of the U.S. press accused Mexican President Calles of sending arms and propaganda to Nicaragua through the intermediary of diplomats of the Soviet Embassy, and in 1928 the government of the United States gave official warning that it would not allow Russian and Mexican soldiers to set up "a soviet in Nicaragua."

The United Press and Associated Press news agencies busied themselves in confirming to the world, through their news reports, the validity of those accusations and fears. Their correspondents in Managua were two North Americans appointed by creditor banks in the United States to take charge of Nicaraguan customs—Clifford Ham of the United Press and Irving Lindbergh of the Associated Press—who spent half their time cheating Nicaragua out of its income from duties and the other half writing up infamies against a bandit named Sandino.

There is nothing new, therefore, in similar derailing maneuvers now being applied by the White House, important news agencies, and the most powerful communications media against Nicaragua.

ALL THE CARNIVAL MASKS ARE NOT ENOUGH

Nicaragua is part of the Third World. Nicaraguans are, therefore, *third-class people.* From the point of view of the opinion makers, they don't deserve respect: *third-class people are condemned to imitate; they have a right to an echo but not to a voice.* For the spokesmen of an international power structure that marginalizes and scorns the majority of humanity, a revolutionary process in a country like Nicaragua can only be attributed to the expansionist drive of the Soviet Union. National dignity and social justice, the cursed history of an occupied country and an exploited people are only pretexts, alibis, decoys for idiots. Everything that is happening in Nicaragua has been reduced to the geopolitics of blocs, a game of East versus West: the blame belongs to Moscow, which is sticking its nose in where it doesn't belong, and, in that way, is changing the delicate balance of power that guarantees world peace. The Contras are not, therefore, merely paid mercenaries working for the restoration of the colonial past and a dethroned dynasty; they aren't Business Fighters, but Freedom Fighters, heroes of a threatened civilization, Western Civilization, which, on the eve of the Apocalypse, turns to God and to the Rambos it can pay.

All the carnival masks in the world are not enough to cover up so much hypocrisy. *Those who deny Nicaragua bread and salt condemn her for receiving them.* The United States was the first country Nicaragua approached in search of commercial credit, development aid, and defensive weapons. The door was slammed in its face. At present, with oil credits from Venezuela and Mexico cut off, Nicaragua depends on the Soviet Union and other countries of the Warsaw Pact for her supply of petroleum and arms. Thanks to arms and petroleum it is surviving. I cannot understand what there is to condemn in assistance for a process of national liberation, nor can I understand why the acceptance of such assistance must turn Nicaragua into a satellite of Moscow.

In any case, Nicaraguans are the first to have an interest in diversifying the sources of economic assistance and they are quite aware that a concentration can involve the danger of political payments. They have always wanted to open up the field, but on the government level, in Western Europe and Latin America, answers of support are becoming more and more infrequent in relation to growing indifference, hostility, and selfishness. Those who condemn Soviet aid in the name of independence would do better to work for some other aid so as to broaden the freedom of movement of this young and besieged revolution.

The revolution, a creative work, doesn't want to apply the Soviet model or any other model. Not even the Cuban model. Foreign models applied to one's own reality end up becoming straitjackets: they propose freedom and end up as restriction. Perhaps Nicaragua wouldn't be alive today if it hadn't been for Cuba's example and generosity. Its supporting hand goes beyond all statistics, past, present, or future, but, as Sergio Ramírez has aptly said, the Sandinistas don't want to make *another Cuba*, but *another Nicaragua.*

THE NECESSARY SATANIZATION

While the president speaks on television from Washington, one feels the map of the Americas being stained red. Nicaragua is pouring out like a torrent of blood: it takes over Central America and Mexico and then enters Texas and continues climbing, climbing—no one can stop it. Will the Big Chief of the Palefaces arrive at a gallop heading up the Fifth Cavalry? Ta-ra-ta-ta, ta-ra-ta-ta, boom, bang, crash: will the red invaders smash into that rocky guardian of Democracy? There he is, front page, there's worry and strength in his face, marked by experience: Ronald Reagan asks to be allowed to act, we still have time, but there isn't much time left, and he reveals a spine-chilling list of horrors committed by the Sandinistas.

The day after the show, a small minority of public opinion in the United States becomes aware of the numerous untruths in the president's speech: no, there's no evidence that the Sandinistas are trafficking in drugs, the federal official specializing in the matter denies this charge; no, it wasn't the Sandinistas who burned down the Managua synagogue, an important rabbi in New York denies that charge also. . . .

For most North Americans, Nicaragua has not been invaded but is the invader; they don't perceive her as a poor colony trying to be a country, but as a mysterious and dangerous power, threatening, lying in wait on the border. Few, very few North Americans have been there and have seen the reality: *that in all of Nicaragua there's only one skyscraper, five elevators, and one escalator (which hasn't worked for over a year), that there are fewer Nicaraguans than there are inhabitants of the borough of Brooklyn in New York, and that because of hunger and disease they live 20 years less than if they'd been born in the United States.*

In his drive to slander Nicaragua, Ronald Reagan has gone to the extreme of being converted, suddenly, to the cause of the Indians. In fact he had already killed plenty of Indians in the movies and was elected president of a country that had killed many more, when he discovered that the Indians of Nicaragua existed. Subsequently he decided to use them as cannon fodder on the military and publicity fronts. While the Sandinistas were teaching the Indians to read and write in their own languages, something never before seen in Nicaragua, and seen few times outside Nicaragua, some of the Indians' principal chiefs were selling out in exchange for goods, or for the promise of a separate nation, and they pushed their people into war. In one of those tragic ironies so frequent in the history of the Americas, many Nicaraguan Indians, condemned from the start to scorn and indifference, have fallen in recent years fighting against the first government that has recognized them as people. In the meantime, official spokesmen of the United States were accusing the Sandinista government of confining the Indians in concentration camps and were circulating photographs of one of their slaughters. The number of Indians presumably imprisoned turned out to be three times greater than the total Indian population, and the photographs turned out to be those of Sandinistas murdered by Somoza's police.

More recently there was a worldwide scandal when two members of the Catholic hierarchy were expelled from Nicaragua for having preached Reagan's lies as though they were God's will. Quite reasonably, President Ortega pointed out that the mass communication media had said little or nothing about the 138 priests murdered and the 268 priests kidnapped in Latin America since 1979, and not a word had been said about the equally eloquent fact that not a single priest had been murdered or kidnapped in Nicaragua during those seven years.

With regard to Reagan's incessant flood of accusations that opinion shapers sell to the world as the revealed truth, Tomás Borge has commented that very soon Nicaragua will also be blamed for AIDS and the devaluation of the dollar. *The fact is, Reagan needs to satanize Nicaragua in order to justify the war economy of the United States.* The fantastic investment in military expenditures give the economy a feeling of prosperity and the citizens a feeling of power, but a spectacular publicity operation is needed in order to maintain them. Nicaragua and Libya afford the alibis of the moment. Daniel Ortega and Muammar Khaddafi play the role of the chief villains in a film full of many other villains who shoot arrows and howl around the Great Stagecoach loaded with bibles and dollars. That film is shown night after night to Western consciousness, so that the armament business has become a natural necessity. Even the stars must be militarized, the United States has decided, in order to confront the terrorist danger. One must attribute to mere chance the coincidence of names between this nation and the nation recently condemned by the World Court in The Hague for its terrorist activities against Nicaragua, one that practices terrorism as an imperial right and that manufactures and exports State terrorism on an industrial scale under the trademark of National Security Policy.

A CRIMINAL SYSTEM

Anyone who dares call things by their names commits the sin of irresponsibility or foolishness. A child has revealed that the emperor has no clothes. The emperor is the all-powerful system that organizes the despoilment of the world and, through unequal exchange and financial extortion, makes it possible for the United States, which has five percent of the world's population, to usurp and ruin the resources of the planet. The history of that system, the history of capitalism, is this history of cannibalism. It is a criminal system. The Bible, which President Reagan so often likes to quote , in a passage Reagan never quotes, says something like: "The bread of the poor is their life. Whosoever taketh it away from them is stained with blood" (Ecclesiastes, 34:21). Nicaragua is not looking for walls to hide behind, but it needs shields with which to defend itself. The victims are rising up against that system during these days of great rebellions, "for it is better to die in battle than for us to stand watching the misfortunes of our nation" (Maccabees, 3:59).

A CHILD LOST IN THE STORM
1990

Lenin's statue removed by a crane in Bucharest. An eager multitude lined up outside McDonald's in Moscow. The odious· Berlin Wall for sale in souvenir-sized chunks. In Warsaw and Budapest, the ministers of economy talking exactly like Margaret Thatcher. And in Beijing, too, as tanks crush students. The Italian Communist Party, largest in the West, announcing its forthcoming suicide. Soviet aid to Ethiopia cut back and Colonel Mengistu suddenly discovering that capitalism is good. The Sandinistas, mainstay of the finest revolution in the world, lose the elections, the headlines proclaiming: "The revolution in Nicaragua falls."

It seems that there is no place for revolutions anymore other than in archeological museum display cases, nor room for the left, except the repentant left willing to sit at the right of the bankers. We are all invited to the world burial of socialism. All of humanity is in the funeral procession, they claim.

I must confess, I don't believe it. This funeral has mistaken the corpse.

IN NICARAGUA, THE JUST PAY FOR THE SINNERS

Perestroika and the passion for freedom unleashed by perestroika have everywhere burst the seams of an unbearable straitjacket. Everything is exploding. Changes proliferating at a dizzying pace founded on the certainty that there is no reason why social justice should be the enemy of freedom or efficiency. An urgency, a collective necessity: The people at the end of their rope, the people fed to the teeth with a bureaucracy as powerful as it was futile, that forbade them in the name of Marx to say what they thought, to live what they felt. Spontaneity of any kind could be considered treason or insanity.

Socialism, communism? Was it all nothing but a historical fraud? I write from a Latin American viewpoint and say to myself: If that was the case, or might have been, why should we be the ones to pay for the fraud? Our face was never in that mirror.

National dignity lost the battle in the recent Nicaraguan elections. It was vanquished by hunger and war: but it was vanquished as well by the international winds that are buffeting the left with greater fury than ever. Unjustly, the just paid for the sinners. The Sandinistas are not to blame either for the war or the hunger. Nor do they bear the slightest reponsibility for what happened in Eastern Europe.

Paradox of paradoxes: A democratic, pluralistic, independent revolution that borrowed nothing from the Soviets, the Chinese, the Cubans or anyone else, has paid for the crockery broken by others, while the local Communist Party voted for Violeta Chamorro.

Those responsible for the war and the hunger are now celebrating the outcome of an election that punishes the victims. The day after it, the U.S. government announced the end of the economic embargo against Nicaragua. This was precisely what happened years ago at the time of the military coup in Chile. The day after President Allende's death, as if by magic, the price of copper rose on the world market.

Actually, the revolution that overthrew the Somoza family dictatorship did not have a moments respite over these last 10 years. It was invaded on a daily basis by a foreign power and its hired criminals and underwent at the same time the relentless pressure of a state of siege on the part of the bankers and commercial masters of the world.

In spite of all this, it managed to be a more civilized revolution than the French Revolution, not having guillotined or stood anyone against the wall, and a more tolerant one than that of the United States, having granted freedom of expression to the local spokespeople of the colonial overlord.

The Sandinistas brought literacy to Nicaragua, significantly reduced infant mortality, and distributed land to the peasantry. But the country was bled white by war. War damage amounted to one-and-a-half times the gross domestic product which means that Nicaragua was destroyed one-and-a-half times. The magistrates of the International Court of Justice in The Hague found against the United States, but its decision had no effect. Nor were the congratulations of the United Nations' specialized organizations for education, food, and health of any avail. Praise is inedible.

The invaders rarely attacked military objectives. Farm cooperatives were their favorite targets. How many thousands of Nicaraguans were killed or wounded on orders of the U.S. government over the past decade? Proportionately, the number would come to 3 million North Americans. Yet many thousands of North Americans visited Nicaragua, were always welcome and nothing ever happened to any of them. Only one died. He was killed by the Contras. (He was very young, an engineer and a clown. Everywhere he went a swarm of children followed him. He organized the first Clown School in Nicaragua. The Contras killed him as he was measuring the water in a lake for a reservoir that was being built. His name was Ben Linder.)

NEW TIMES, TWO SIDES OF THE COIN

The U.S. government invokes democracy with respect to Panama, Nicaragua, or Cuba the way the Eastern European governments invoked socialism—as an alibi. Latin America has been invaded by the United States more than a hundred times in this century. Always in the name of democracy and always to impose military dictatorships or puppet governments that safeguarded endangered money. The imperial power system does not want democracies: It wants humbled countries.

The invasion of Panama was scandalous, with its 7,000 victims among the ruins of the poor barrios leveled by the bombings. But more scandalous than the invasions was the impunity with which it was effected. Impunity, which encourages repetition of a misdeed, stimulates the delinquent. French President Mitterrand greeted this crime of sovereignty with discreet applause, and the whole world sat back—after a tithe of a statement had been paid here and there.

In this context, silence and even thinly disguised complacence on the part of some of the Eastern European countries speaks eloquently. Does the liberation there give the green light to oppression of the West? I never went along with the attitude of those who condemned imperialism in the Caribbean but applauded or kept their mouths shut when sovereignty was trampled in Hungary, Poland, Czechoslovakia, or Afghanistan.

I can say this because I have never operated under a double standard: The right of self-determination of nations is sacred in all places at all times. It is well said by those who point out that Gorbachev's democratic reforms were possible because the Soviet Union ran no risk of being invaded by the Soviet Union; and in parallel, by those who point out that the United States is safe from coups and military dictatorships because there is no U.S. Embassy in the United States.

Without a shadow of a doubt, freedom is always good news. For the East European countries now enjoying it and for the entire world. But at the same time, are the paeans to money and the virtues of the marketplace good news? The idolatry of the American way of life? The naive illusion of an invitation to membership in the International Club for the Rich? The bureaucracy, nimble only for stepping into better positions, is rapidly adapting to the new situation and the old bureaucrats are beginning to transform themselves into a new bourgeoisie.

It must be understood that from the standpoint of Latin America and the so-called Third World, the defunct Soviet bloc had at least one fundamental virtue: It did not get fat by feeding off the poor, did not take part in the raping by the international capitalist market. On the contrary, it helped to fund justice in Cuba, Nicaragua and many other countries. I suspect that in the not very distant future this will be remembered with nostalgia.

A Nightmare Come True

For us, capitalism is not a dream to be made a reality, but a nightmare come true. Our challenge lies not in privatizing the state but in deprivatizing it. Our states have been bought at bargain prices by the those who own the land, the banks, and everything else. And for us, the market is nothing more than a pirate ship—the greater its freeedom, the worse its behavior. The local market and the world market. The world market robs us with both hands. The commercial arm keeps charging us more and more for what it sells us and paying less and less for what it buys. The financial arm that lends us our own money keeps paying us less and charging us more.

We live in a region where European prices and African wages prevail, where capitalism acts like the kind man who said, "I'm so fond of poor people that it seems to me there are never enough of them." In Brazil alone, for example, the system kills 1,000 children a day by disease or starvation.

With or without elections, capitalism in Latin America is antidemocratic—most of the people are prisoners of need, doomed to isolation and violence. Hunger lies, violence lies:

They claim that they are part of nature; they feign belonging to the natural order of things. When that "natural order" grows disorderly, the military comes on the scene, hooded or barefaced. As they say in Colombia: "The more the cost of living goes up, the less life is worth."

The elections in Nicaragua were a very cruel blow. A blow like hatred from God, as the poet said. When I heard the result, I was, and still am, a child lost in the storm. A child lost, yes, but not alone. We are many. Throughout the world, we are many.

Step by Step

I sometimes feel as though they have stolen even our words. The term "socialist" is applied in the West as the false face of injustice; in the East, it evokes purgatory or perhaps hell. The world "imperialism" is out of style and no longer to be found in the dominant political lexicon, even though imperialism is present and does pillage and kill. And the term "militancy"? And the very fact of militant fervor? For the theoreticians of disenchantment it is a ridiculous old relic. For the repentant, a memory disturbance.

In a few months we have witnessed the turbulent shipwreck of a system that usurped socialism, that treated the people like a child that never grew up, and dragged it along by the ear. Three or four centuries ago, the Inquisitors slandered God by saying that they were carrying out his orders; but I believe that Christianity is not the Holy Inquisition. In our time, the bureaucrats have stigmatized hope and befouled the most beautiful of human adventures; but I also believe that socialism is not Stalinism.

Now, we must begin all over again. Step by step, with no shields but those born of our own bodies. It is necessary to discover, create, imagine. In a speech shortly after his defeat, Jesse Jackson championed the right to dream: "Let us defend that right," he said. "Let us not permit anybody to take that right from us." And today more than ever it is necessary to dream. To dream, together, dreams that undream themselves and become incarnate in mortal matter, as was said, wished, by another poet. My friends live fighting for that right, and have given their lives for it, some of them.

This is my testimony. A dinosaur's confession? Perhaps. In any case, it is the affirmation of one who believes that the human condition is not doomed to selfishness and the obscene pursuit of money, and that socialism did not die, because it had not yet been—that today is the first day in the long life it has yet to live.

1979

Managua. July 20, 1979,
tens of thousands pack the
Plaza de la República,
renamed Plaza de la
Revolución, in celebration
of the popular insurrection
that overthrew dictator
Anastasio Somoza Debayle.

Under a scorching tropical sun they danced: tens of thousands of peasants and students, factory workers and their bosses. They sang, laughed, waved flags and embraced. Above the din could be heard a constant chant, "The people united will never be defeated." It was Managua, July 20, 1979, and 45 years of dictatorship were over.

Only months earlier, Anastasio Somoza and his brutal Guardia Nacional had gripped Nicaragua in a vise of terror, and only few had dared believe they could be beaten. At the start of 1978, the Sandinista National Liberation Front, the FSLN, numbered fewer than 1,500 ragged guerrillas. But the Frente, as the FSLN was also known, forged a pragmatic alliance with the country's wealthy business class and galvanized the urban poor. By the time Somoza fled, the ranks of Sandinista guerrillas had grown perhaps tenfold, and were backed by thousands of supporters who built barricades, supplied food and intelligence, and manufactured bombs.

The victorious Sandinistas' ambitions went beyond transforming the lives of the poor. They wanted to make Nicaragua a model for a new Latin America. They dreamed of reaching out to Africa and other parts of the Third World to end the traditional dominance of the developed countries. They challenged sexism, and encouraged women's rights. Above all, they were determined to resist any interference from the United States, and to protect Nicaraguan sovereignty at all costs.

But Nicaragua was in desperate straits. Somoza had left just $3.5 million in the treasury. The 1972 earthquake and two years of war had decimated industry and agriculture. There were 150,000 war wounded and only 5,000 hospital beds in the entire country. Forty thousand children were orphans, and half a million people were homeless. Average life expectancy was only 53 years, and infant mortality was 12 percent; while more than half the country was illiterate and earned less than $300 a year. There was no parliament, no functioning bureaucracy, no police force, no army, no judges. To cap it all, weeks after "the Triumph" of the revolution, gun battles continued to rock city nights, as embittered Guardias emerged from hiding to attack the Sandinistas.

Elsewhere, an extraordinary new community spirit prevailed. Thousands of people volunteered weekends and evenings to clear war ruins and build roads and parks. The unity was reflected in the new governing Junta, composed of three Sandinistas, and two representatives of the conservative business class—Violeta Chamorro, widow of the owner of the newspaper *La Prensa*, and millionaire industrialist Alfonso Robelo, whose supporters filled many positions in the fledgling bureaucracy.

In an effort to jump start the economy, young Sandinistas bounced around the country in rusty jeeps or camped out in ramshackle offices, working non-stop to build a new society. A sort of anarchic idealism prevailed. Meanwhile the inspirational victory over Somoza and the hope that the country could become an example to the rest of the Third World led to an outpouring of international aid: about $1.2 billion within the first year, including a promised $75 million from the U.S.

Managua. Toppled statue of Anastasio Somoza García, founder of the Somoza dynasty, being dragged through the streets.

Matagalpa. Neighborhood volunteers clear the streets of war rubble. Somoza's air force bombed neighborhoods and factories, contributing to an estimated $480 million worth of war damage.

Estelí. A boy with a wooden gun emulates Sandinista fighters.

San Marcos. Peasants examine a television
confiscated from their former landowner.

Downtown Managua.

Despite millions of dollars in international donations sent to the Somoza government, the center of the city was never rebuilt after the devastating earthquake of 1972.

1980

Carazo Department. Peasants on their way to take over unused land carry a banner reading "We are not birds that live in the air, nor fish that live in the sea. We are men who live from the land."

*Managua. Sandinista police celebrate the first
anniversary of the triumph over Somoza.*

On August 23, more than 250,000 people packed Managua's main square to welcome home 70,000 exultant Literacy Crusade volunteers. The wildly successful campaign had been a radicalizing experience for urban middle-class youths who had "gone to the mountain" and discovered their country's natural wealth as well as the poverty of the peasantry. The Crusade also symbolized the government's resolve to spread the fruits of revolution. The first priority was rapid social change.

To reduce unemployment, labor-intensive road, sewage, and construction projects were launched. Rural health clinics were built, paramedics trained, and medical coverage was expanded from 30 percent to the whole population. Buildings seized from Somoza and his supporters became retirement homes and orphanages. Urban rents were halved.

But political tensions were mounting. Thousands of conservatives fled, taking with them machinery, livestock, and millions of dollars. The Junta responded by legislating against decapitalization and allowing peasants to occupy idle farmland—actions the fragmented opposition saw as attacks on private property. The conservatives were convinced that the FSLN would try to impose a one-party system, and bitterly criticized its control of the Sandinista People's Army, the police, and both TV channels.

The Sandinistas, mindful of the U.S. Central Intelligence Agency's history of destabilizing leftist Latin American governments, were determined to prevent opponents from using the media or armed forces to undermine the revolution. Despite U.S. accusations, pluralism had always been part of the FSLN platform. Nationalizing the entire economy would have financially crippled its plans for social change and risked U.S. intervention. It accepted opposition parties that would operate within the emerging revolutionary constitutional framework, and tried to work with the private sector; between 1980-82, 54 % of all low-interest, government-approved loans went to private producers.

In April, the Junta announced the composition of the consultative Council of State. Before the Triumph, conservatives had hoped for a majority. Instead they received only 11 seats out of 47, while the FSLN took 24. Robelo and Chamorro resigned from the Junta, and only intense negotiations prevented a boycott of the assembly by the businessmen's organization COSEP.

At the Literacy Crusade homecoming, Defense Minister Humberto Ortega, brother of Junta Coordinator Daniel Ortega, announced that elections would not be held until 1985. Conservatives were horrified. Increased demand, idle farms, and panic buying led to food shortages. The FSLN accused *La Prensa* and COSEP of using scare tactics, and started to censor what it considered economic disinformation.

In November, Sandinista youths ransacked Robelo's party offices. COSEP delegates then walked out of the Council of State, never to return. A week later, COSEP's most charismatic leader, Jorge Salazar, was shot dead while allegedly resisting arrest. The death of Salazar, who was accused of plotting a coup and smuggling weapons into the country, convinced many conservatives that working with the Sandinistas was impossible.

Managua. Market vendors learning to write their names.
Nearby hangs a poster of Nicaraguan national hero Augusto
César Sandino who, from 1927-1933, fought against the
U.S. Marines who occupied the country.

Matagalpa Department. Literacy class at El Roblar farm cooperative.

The nationwide literacy campaign of 1980 cut illiteracy from 51 to 13 percent. Urban middle-class youths, many of whom had not taken part in combat against Somoza, were inspired by their experiences as volunteer literacy teachers in remote rural villages and became engaged in the goals of the revolution. Returning to the cities, they spread their enthusiasm to family members, extending Sandinista support. The campaign earned Nicaragua a United Nations award.

Managua. Street celebration.

Managua. A main intersection in the capital.

*Managua. Street corner marked by a monument
to two martyrs of the revolution.*

*Masaya. A wedding party promenades past a billboard
calling for "communal solutions to social problems."*

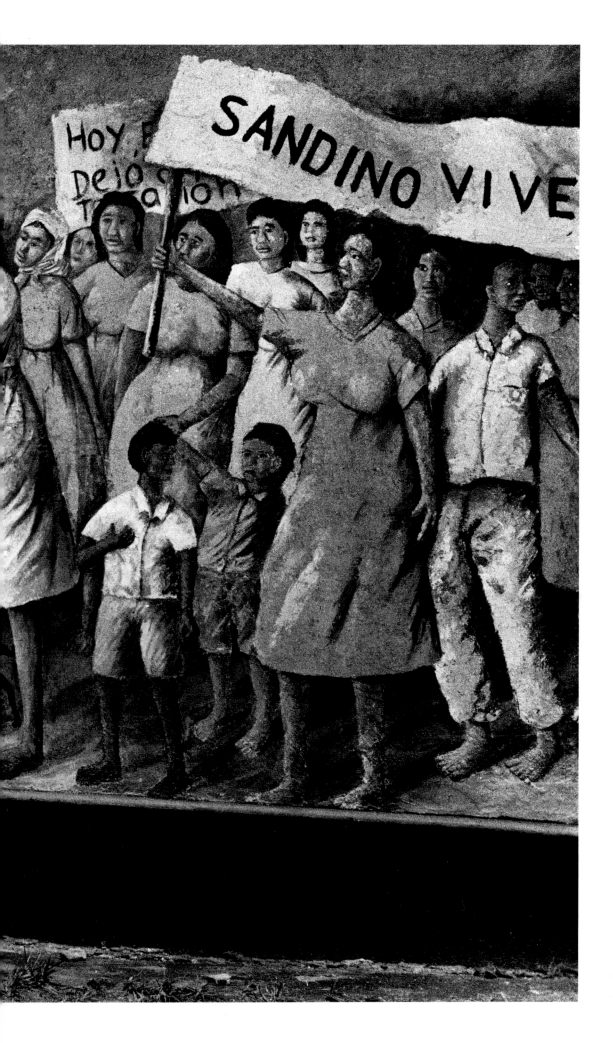

Managua. Revolutionary mural.

*International artists' brigades
joined Nicaraguan artists
to paint murals throughout
the country.*

1981

*San José de Cusmapa.
Peasants receive arms for
defense against possible
Contra attacks.*

In January, Ronald Wilson Reagan was inaugurated President of the United States. No other event in the 1980's was to have as profound an effect on Nicaragua. Reagan's fiercely anticommunist administration was determined to "roll back" a Marxist state, and Nicaragua became the principal testing ground for the strategy of "low-intensity conflict," designed to overthrow a foreign government without committing U.S. troops.

The new president immediately froze all aid to Nicaragua, including food credits, and ordered his representatives to veto all international loans to the country. The first casualty was a loan to build rural roads that would help peasants get crops to market. Over the next four years, annual multilateral aid fell from $110 million to zero. On March 9, Reagan signed a secret "finding" authorizing CIA operations against Nicaragua. The Agency, with Argentine support, moved quickly to recruit and train former Guardia to create an anti-Sandinista guerrilla force—the Contras.

Meanwhile, Nicaragua's economy was booming; over the next three years it would grow faster than any other in Latin America. There were huge strides in health and education, housing construction, and electrification. Per capita consumption of pork and rice was up 60% over 1977, and few children could be seen begging or selling cigarettes on the streets. In July, a revolutionary hero tested the popular loyalty to the Sandinistas—and lost: Edén Pastora, one of the leaders of the insurrection, became disenchanted and fled into exile, hoping to divide the army and challenge the FSLN leadership. Crowds of people responded by demonstrating and tearing up their militia cards signed by Pastora.

Yet the first complaints could be heard on the streets, especially about food shortages. Too much money was chasing too few goods; generous credits to peasants and the wages of thousands of new government workers boosted the demand for cheap subsidized food. Rationing was introduced, run by Sandinista Defense Committees, neighborhood organizations which opponents argued were used to coerce their silence. Banks and foreign trade had been nationalized—effectively giving the government the power to control private businesses, by deciding which farms or factories would get dollars to buy seeds or machinery and what price they would be paid for their crops and products. COSEP complained that red tape and political antagonism were delaying credits and wrecking their businesses, and capital flight continued.

By mid-year, 30 percent of the land was idle as owners either emigrated or waited out political developments. On July 19, the Sandinistas announced the Agrarian Reform law, designed to affect only the largest estates and only those that were abandoned or unproductive. The confiscated land was to be given to cooperatives and to individual peasants, as well as to expand the state farms that had been carved out of Somoza's holdings.

In August, Reagan sent an envoy with a brash ultimatum: peaceful relations in return for a quota of power for conservatives. The Sandinistas refused. The next month, in a blatant display of intimidation, joint U.S.–Honduran military maneuvers started north of the border. In November Reagan, with Congressional acquiescence, approved nearly $20 million for the Contras.

Estelí Department. Members of the El Coyolito farm cooperative pile harvested corn.

Estelí Department. El Coyolito agricultural cooperative.

*Matagalpa Department. Communal kitchen at
La Lucha state coffee farm.*

*Matagalpa Department. In a barn at La Estrella state farm,
a worker sorts coffee beans while children attend class.*

*Matagalpa Department.
Packing coffee at a
farm cooperative.*

*In 1979, the new government
confiscated Somoza's vast
agricultural holdings, equal-
ling 20 percent of all arable
land. Initially, the agrarian
reform program created large
state farms. That policy
began to change in 1981 to
emphasize cooperatives, and
later, individual ownership.
By 1985, more than 65,000
farmers had received titles
to their own lands.*

Pantipitu, Río Grande de Matagalpa. Village portrait.

Pantipitu, Río Grande de Matagalpa. Village volunteers build a schoolhouse.

Pantipitu, Río Grande de Matagalpa. A farmer practices his writing.

Tumarín, Río Grande de Matagalpa. Dugout canoes.

1982

Matagalapa Department. Telephone workers string a line through the jungle, connecting Nicaragua's Atlantic and Pacific coasts for the first time.

Matagalpa Department. Health brigade volunteer vaccinates a coffee picker against polio.

In 1982, a national healthcare campaign eradicated polio and dramatically reduced the incidence of other diseases, such as malaria.

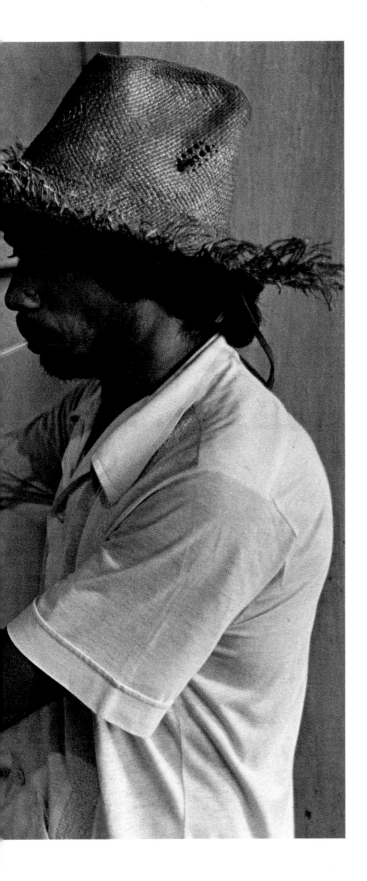

On March 14, Contra saboteurs, trained by the CIA, blew up two important bridges near the Honduran border. Although isolated attacks by former Guardia had continued since 1979, this operation effectively marked the start of the Contra war in the populous northwestern region of Nicaragua. The next day, the Junta declared a state of emergency. The country polarized rapidly. Robelo and his supporters chose self-imposed exile; and within a year they joined Edén Pastora to create their own guerrilla army, ARDE, operating from Costa Rica.

Uncertain whom to trust, and fearing internal destabilization, the Sandinistas moved to control their domestic opponents. They extended censorship to cover all news, and conservative leaders were harassed. In the countryside, overzealous Sandinista security agents began picking up anyone who looked suspicious. Some suspects were beaten, others held without trial for several weeks.

On the Atlantic Coast, events spiraled out of control. The Sandinistas arrived in 1979 determined to bring the benefits of social and economic progress, and built the first land route to the isolated region. But they demonstrated little understanding of the black Creole or Miskito Indian communities. When Miskito leaders started a secessonist movement, they were jailed. After their release they fled to Honduras, and in late 1981 launched an assault that became known as "Red Christmas."

It was the first concerted military attack on the revolution, and the army overreacted. In January, the Sandinistas decided to move all the Miskito communities from their traditional homeland along the Río Coco. Some 8,500 Indians were marched 40 miles inland to stark resettlement areas carved out of the jungle. Behind them, Sandinista troops torched their homes, churches, and crops. Later in the year, another 7,000 Indians suffered the same fate. In the process, about 50 Miskitos disappeared.

Meanwhile, the Catholic church hierarchy began using its influence against the government. The Sandinistas had endorsed the Popular Church, a fusion of Marxism and Christianity, based on liberation theology, which was dividing the church throughout the continent. Much of the government's support came from within the Popular Church, and four priests were members of the government cabinet. When they rejected Archbishop Miguel Obando y Bravo's call to resign from the government, he expelled pro-Sandinista priests from their parishes. Some parishoners who opposed Obando responded by occupying their churches, while gangs of youths heckled and jostled the bishops.

These developments led international human rights organizations to criticize the revolution for the first time, after they had initially praised it for abolishing the death penalty and for avoiding a bloodbath of captured Guardia. But loyalty to the revolution and its gains remained strong. Adult education workshops continued the work of the Literacy Crusade, and the school population was now double that of the Somoza era. Food prices and public transport were still subsidized, and telephone workers laid a line through the jungle connecting the two halves of the country for the first time. Thousands of volunteers reported for militia training and were organized into reserve battalions.

Catarina. Festival honoring the town's patron saint.

Yalí. Schoolroom at La Primavera agricultural cooperative.

Rama. Sandinista Defense Committee slogan stenciled on a wall of the town telephone office reads "All the People to the Militias."

TODO
EL PUEBLO
A LAS
MILICIAS

COMITES DE
DEFENSA C.D.S.
SANDINISTA

Nicarao base, Honduran-Nicaraguan border. Raw recruits undergo their first days of training with the Contras at a base camp northeast of Ocotal.

Northern Nicaragua. Contras advance on a hamlet of 12 houses.

Tasba Pri. Miskito Indian family at a relocation camp in northeastern Nicaragua. More than 15,000 Indians were forcibly resettled inland after fighting broke out between Miskito rebels and Sandinistas along the Río Coco.

1983

Río San Juan.
Sandinista troops on patrol.

Once again a packed Managua square witnessed the drama of revolution. On March 4, Pope John Paul II stood before a crowd of 750,000 and delivered a stern lecture condemning the Popular Church and its "unacceptable ideological commitments"—commitments, he meant, to the FSLN. Sandinistas in the crowd began to drown his voice with chants of "We want peace." The Mass ended in chaos, with the church hierarchy now firmly in the opposition camp.

The pace of war was accelerating dramatically. At Nicaragua's urging, Venezuela, Colombia, Panama, and Mexico created the Contadora Group, which tried to orchestrate a dialogue between the U.S. and the Sandinistas. It was an attempt to reverse the historical dominance of the U.S. over regional events, but instead of negotiation, Washington responded with a series of intimidating moves. In February, the Pentagon mounted huge military maneuvers in Honduras near the Nicaraguan border—including a simulated invasion of a fictitious Central American nation. In July, the aircraft carrier *Ranger* and its battle group appeared off the Nicaraguan coast. In September, the largest maneuvers in Central America's history were held in Honduras as the battleship *New Jersey* steamed offshore. In October high-speed motorboats manned by CIA "assets" attacked and partially destroyed oil installations at Corinto and Puerto Sandino.

Military officers from El Salvador, Honduras, Guatemala, and Panama discussed the possibility of joint intervention to support a Contra "provisional government." Meanwhile, Pentagon radio traffic created the impression that an assault might be in the offing. The U.S. invasion of Grenada in October convinced many Sandinistas that direct intervention in Nicaragua was a real and immediate threat. All over the capital people started digging trenches. TV spots showed how to fire a rifle and build a bomb shelter. Supermarket shelves were stripped bare. Even foreign embassies discussed evacuation plans.

At the same time the Junta introduced compulsory military service. Previously, the army had relied on volunteer militia and reserve units, composed mainly of supporters from the urban workforce and former guerrilla fighters. Now the Sandinistas decided that any war casualties should not be borne solely by their supporters. Thousands of middle-class youths fled into exile, and the church mounted a campaign encouraging draft resistance. Compulsory military service would ultimately prove to be the Sandinistas' most politically damaging decision.

In November, hoping to defuse tensions with the U.S., the Junta ordered Salvadoran guerrillas to dismantle their Managua-based high command and leave the country. A thousand Cuban military advisers returned home; censorship was suddenly relaxed and elections were announced for 1984. Finally, the Sandinistas submitted a proposal to the Contadora Group offering major concessions on U.S. security concerns. But hardliners in Washington rejected any negotiated settlement. Although the World Health Organization declared that Nicaragua was now a model for health care in Latin America, the Sandinistas had no time to celebrate. They were focused on the war, which was now in full swing.

Planes de Vilán, Jinotega Department. A peasant killed by Contra rebels lies amidst the ruins of his farm cooperative.

Managua. Mothers plead with Pope John Paul II to bless their sons killed fighting the Contras. When the Pope ignored the women, the crowd echoed their request until, apparently irate, he shouted, "Silence! Silence!"

56

Managua. The Pope admonishes Father Ernesto Cardenal, Nicaraguan Minister of Culture, for disobeying papal orders to resign his post in the Sandinista government.

Corinto. More than 3 million gallons of gasoline and other fuel go up in flames after storage tanks are sabotaged by CIA-trained commandos, or UCLAS (Unilaterally Controlled Latin Assets); 25,000 local residents were evacuated.

Jinotega Department. Sandinista soldier during combat.

Managua. Volunteers join the Sandinista Popular Militia.

*Río San Juan Department. A boy about to be relocated
from his home as part of a government program to remove
peasants from war zones in southern Nicaragua.*

*Río San Juan Department. Sandinista soldiers move
peasants from their homes to resettlement camps.*

Río San Juan Department. War resettlement camp.

Jinotega Department.
Classroom in Dantanlí.

During the first four years of the revolution, the number of students almost doubled; the number of teachers working in the schools quadrupled.

Northern Nicaragua. Contras obtain food from local peasants.

Río San Juan Department. Sandinista militia at base camp.

Cerro el Chamarro, Jinotega Department. Sandinista
soldiers with a suspected Contra collaborator.

1984

Nueva Guinea. Peasant farmer at La Unión farm cooperative.

In early January, CIA contract agents in speedboats quietly slipped into Nicaragua's three largest ports and dropped mines onto the seabed. A month later, two Nicaraguan trawlers sank, and in March, ships from the Netherlands, Panama, the Soviet Union, and Japan were damaged. An international outcry-followed; Britain protested, France offered to send minesweepers, and Nicaragua sued the U.S. at the International Court of Justice, forcing Washington into an embarrassing rejection of the court's jurisdiction. U.S. Senator Barry Goldwater, Chairman of the Intelligence Committee, wrote to CIA Director William Casey, saying, "I am pissed off. . . . This is an act violating international law. It is an act of war." In October, the fallout led Congress to pass the Boland amendment, suspending all aid to the Contras.

By now the Contras had gained a reputation for brutality. Instead of targeting the army, they focused on anything or anyone identified with the revolution, including schools, health clinics, cooperatives, nurses, and teachers. The Sandinistas were slow to respond to the Contra threat. Until mid-year, when the new conscript battalions entered the field, the army relied on the militias to face a CIA-backed army built around a core of well-trained ex-Guardia. With the Contras ambushing trucks, blowing up bridges, and destroying farms—and with peasants being drafted to fight the Contras—it became increasingly difficult to harvest the vital coffee crop and get other agricultural products to market. Food shortages worsened, and growing ranks of critics cut into the Sandinistas' still-significant popular support.

With the Contras claiming some 15,000 troops—some of whom had been kidnapped or bribed to join—the Frente continued to search for a negotiated solution. In September, the Sandinistas unconditionally accepted the Contadora Group's proposed regional peace treaty. Despite having initially endorsed the plan, the White House reacted by suddenly demanding that it be redrafted. Meanwhile Nicaragua prepared to elect a new president and National Assembly.The FSLN hoped that democratic elections would convince the United States to leave Nicaragua alone.

Arturo Cruz, the candidate of the main conservative alliance, returned to Nicaragua from his self-imposed exile in Washington. He soon withdrew his candidacy. He argued that the electoral process was unfair, pointing to violence surrounding three campaign rallies at which Sandinista youths clashed with his supporters. On November 4, the FSLN won 67 percent of the vote; six opposition parties shared 29 percent. Foreign observers—including a delegate from the British Conservative party—declared the voting to have been free and fair. But, citing the abstention of Cruz—who, as it later emerged, was in the pay of the CIA—the White House dismissed the results.

Two days later, Reagan was reelected in a 49-state landslide. Even as the results were being announced, U.S. intelligence sources leaked false reports that Soviet MIG fighter aircraft were about to arrive at the port of Corinto. Pentagon officials discussed "surgical strikes," and American supersonic spy planes flew over Nicaragua, leading the Sandinistas to suspect that, flush with victory, Reagan might finally invade.

Condega. San Jerónimo coffee cooperative after Contra attack.

Murra. Funeral for a militia-man killed by Contras.

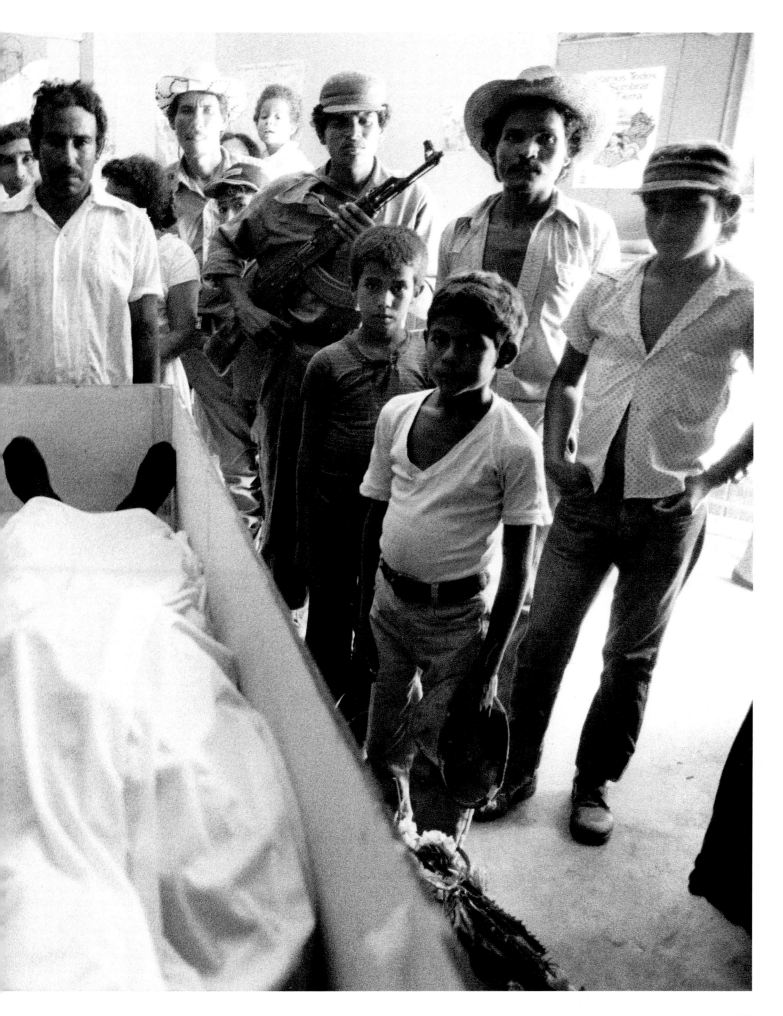

Managua. Preparing for the festival of the Immaculate Conception.

Bluefields. Rehearsal for the Maypole festival.

Masaya. Police block Sandinista supporters known as turbas divinas
or "divine mobs" threatening an opposition campaign rally.

On August 1, 1984, the Nicaraguan government lifted most emergency restrictions and eased press censorship in preparation for elections in November. Junta Coordinator Daniel Ortega led the Sandinista ticket as presidential candidate, with Junta member Sergio Ramírez running for vice president. Ortega and the Sandinistas were victorious, receiving 67 percent of the vote and 61 seats in the new National Assembly, while six opposition parties won 29 percent of the vote and 35 seats.

León. Daniel Ortega and Sergio Ramírez campaigning.

Managua. Sandinista supporters celebrate election victory.

Managua. Preparing to defend against U.S. invasion.

Towards the year's end, the announcement of new U.S.–sponsored military maneuvers in the region and the Reagan administration's increased threats against the Sandinista government heightened Nicaraguans' fear of invasion. The Sandinistas deployed tanks, mobilized militias and resumed the state of emergency.

1985

Managua. A member of the neighborhood defense committee distributes rationed soap, cooking oil, rice, and beans.

The war economy brought about a great scarcity of basic goods; at the same time, it forced the government to cut food subsidies.

Managua. After losing a leg to a Contra mine in Mulukukú,
a young boy waits at a rehabilitation center.

On January 10, Daniel Ortega was sworn in as Nicaragua's first democratically elected president. At Washington's behest, few foreign governments sent high-level representatives to the ceremony. Reagan dismissed the election results and continued his destabilization efforts.

However, there was encouraging news for the Sandinistas on the war front: the so-called MIG fighters that arrived in November proved to be deadly MI-25 attack helicopters. They played a key role in turning the war around, enabling the army to hit the Contras every time they regrouped. And the conscript Irregular Warfare Battalions sprang into action. These well-armed, well-trained, and highly motivated troops proved devastatingly effective, and by year's end they would succeed in driving many of the Contras back to their bases in Honduras.

But the introduction of what the Frente called Patriotic Military Service led Archbishop Obando y Bravo to question the government's legitimacy and declare, "The attitude for those who oppose the Sandinista ideology must be that of conscientious objection." In April, the Pope rewarded Obando by elevating him to Cardinal. On his way home from Rome, Obando stopped in Miami to celebrate a Mass attended by top Contra leaders. In Managua, he became the symbolic leader of all opposition to the revolution. With his encouragement, mothers protested in the streets and fought army recruiters, while some priests hid draft dodgers.

There was also a major change in agrarian reform policies. Contra attacks had so devastated the cooperatives that crop production plummeted. In response, the government decided to speed up land distribution to individual peasants—hoping to cement their support, while easing the Contra threat to the co-ops. In the mountains, the army created free-fire zones by relocating 7,000 isolated farmers, many of whom were suspected Contra sympathizers. The resettlement camps had the advantages of schools and health care but in turn became targets for Contra attacks.

In April, the U.S. Congress voted down all Contra aid. In May, Reagan struck back: Nicaragua represented such an "unusual and extraordinary security threat," he said, that he was obliged to declare a national emergency in order to prohibit all trade between the two countries. The Sandinistas had anticipated the move but could not avert the major economic dislocation it caused. Reagan's rhetoric grew more vitriolic: Nicaragua was a "totalitarian dungeon," Ortega a "tin-pot dictator," and the Contras "the moral equivalent of the Founding Fathers."

At the same time, under intense U.S. pressure, Mexico halted oil deliveries to Nicaragua. Ortega rushed to Moscow to secure an alternative supply, but in Washington the trip appeared to prove Nicaragua's communist leanings. As a result, in June Congress approved $27 million in "non-lethal" aid to the Contras.

The war economy became a way of life. Social spending was cut for the first time; health care suffered the most. Food became scarcer and more costly as subsidies were removed. The slogan painted everywhere was "No Pasarán"—They shall not pass—and as more people received weapons and training, the country became, in the Sandinistas' words, "a people in arms."

Managua. Baseball game inside the ruins of the metropolitan cathedral, destroyed by the 1972 earthquake.

Managua. Monument to the revolution.

Juigalpa. Celebrating mass on the traditional Day of the Dead.

Managua. Factory employees learn to handle weapons for national defense.

Managua. Sandinista celebration.

*Waspam. Miskito Indians gaze at the Río Coco, which divides
Nicaragua from Honduras, after returning to their homes.*

In 1985, after more than three years of warfare between Sandinista forces and Miskito rebels, the Nicaraguan government signed truces with several Miskito Indian guerrilla commanders. The Sandinisitas admitted past mistakes, offered regional autonomy and allowed thousands of the Indians to leave resettlement camps and return to their ancestral homes.

Saupuka. Miskitos sing at a religious celebration upon their return home.

La Trinidad.
Dead Contra soldiers.

The Contra attack and
occupation of this town just
55 miles from Managua,
served as notice that the
rebels would no longer be
confined to border areas but
would strike inland as well.

91

Managua. Shoppers line up for shoes.

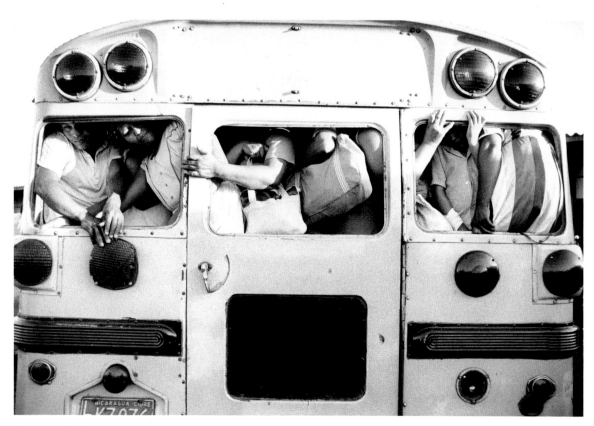

Managua. Public bus.

Managua. Anti-government protesters clash with police at a May Day march.

The U.S. trade embargo against Nicaragua created a shortage of mechanical spare parts and supplies; at the same time, the Contra war produced a flood of migration from rural areas to the cities. Managua became home to one-third of the country's population, contributing to a crisis in public transportation, water supplies, and other public services. Combined with shortages of food and other commodities, these pressures increased political divisions in the country.

1986

San José de Bocay.
A funeral procession for
32 civilians killed when
the truck they rode in struck
a Contra land mine.

In May, the second-largest Contra army, Edén Pastora's Costa Rican–based ARDE, formally disbanded. It was the first public confirmation of the Sandinistas' mounting military successes. Once, ARDE had controlled much of the southeast, but in 1985 Sandinista troops had captured every ARDE base inside Nicaragua.

In the meantime, the Sandinistas negotiated with rebel leaders on the Atlantic Coast, admitting their mistakes and offering regional autonomy to the Miskitos and Creoles. It was a bold strategy and risked dismembering the nation, but it worked: by 1986 many Miskito guerrillas had hung up their rifles. With these successes the army was able to focus on the northwest, where the main Contra units now operated.

In June, the World Court found the U.S. guilty of violating international law for mining Nicaraguan harbors in 1984. Still Reagan would not relent. In August Congress bowed to presidential pressure and approved $100 million in new military aid for the Contras. This was more than enough to revitalize the rebels. Soon heavily armed units, with computerized communications equipment and shoulder-launched antiaircraft weapons, would begin moving back across the border from Honduras.

The Sandinistas reacted with their strongest measures yet. Calling the aid a declaration of war, they closed *La Prensa* and the Catholic radio station. Opposition leaders, many of whom had called on the U.S. Congress to approve Contra aid, were harrassed, arrested, or expelled. The punitive measures undermined the revolution's image abroad, leading some to believe Reagan's claim that the Sandinistas were repressive and dictatorial.

But on October 5, the entire U.S. strategy began to unravel. Sandinista troops shot down a C-123 cargo plane, and one of its crew, former U.S. Marine Eugene Hasenfus, was captured. Hasenfus said he was part of a CIA arms-delivery operation, an activity expressly forbidden by Congress since 1984. Documents retrieved from the plane seemed to back his story and gave evidence of Lt. Col. Oliver North's covert Contra-supply operation.

On November 25, U.S. Attorney General Edwin Meese was forced to reveal that missiles had been sold to Iran and the proceeds illegally used to buy arms for the Contras. During the subsequent investigation it emerged that the Contras had exaggerated their numbers and capacity; that their tactics were dominated by efforts to win support in Washington, rather than to defeat the Nicaraguan army; that reforms meant to improve their abysmal human-rights record were largely cosmetic; and that they may have engaged in drug running to finance their activities.

The revelations hurt the Contras, but by now much of the damage to the country had been done. Contra attacks had closed many coffee farms in the north and forced the government to use valuable cotton estates in safe coastal areas to grow food that could no longer be farmed in the mountains. The trade embargo meant the fishing fleet and industry were grinding to a halt for lack of spare parts. As exports collapsed, the FSLN found it increasingly difficult to obtain foreign loans, because security measures used to contain the Contra threat looked repressive. And the new Contra aid threatened to restart the whole vicious cycle.

Managua. Supermarket.

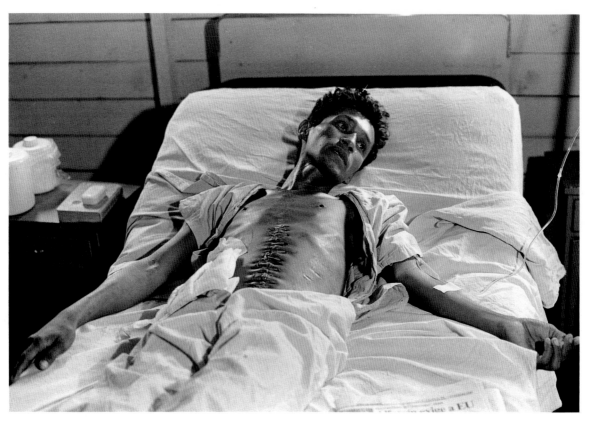

*Jinotega Department. A wounded Sandinista
soldier in Apanás Military Hospital.*

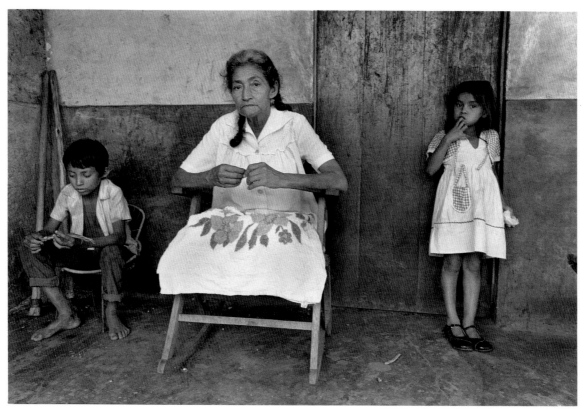

*Pantasma. Children with their grandmother, who
lost her legs in a Contra mine explosion.*

San José de Bocay. Mass burial for the
32 victims of the Contra land mine.

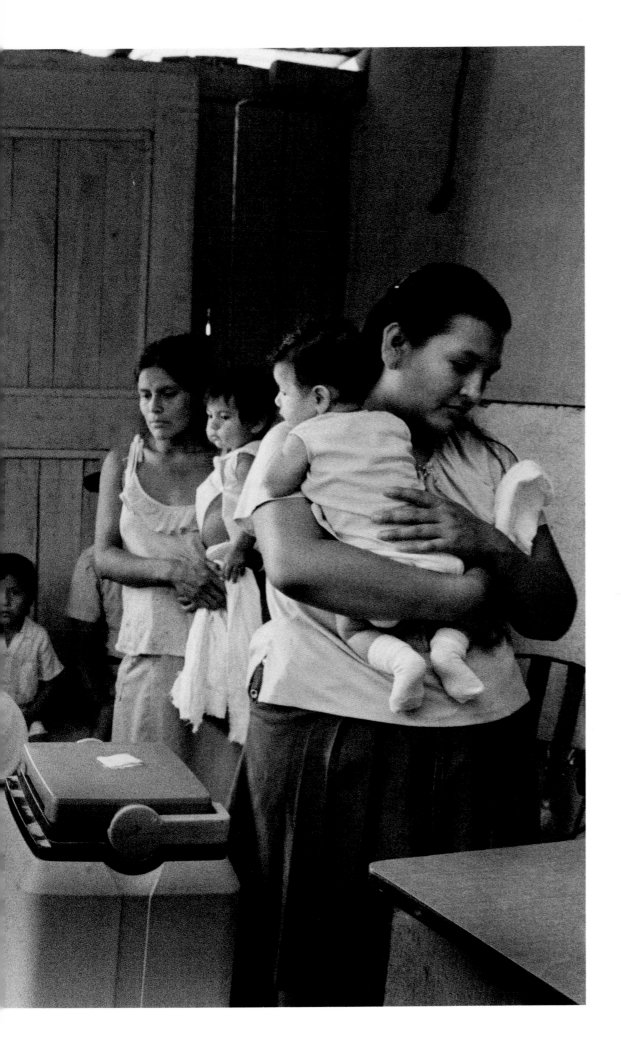

Managua. Polio vaccination.

Throughout Nicaragua the government attempted to maintain social and health programs it had established over the years. However the war made it difficult for medical workers to travel to remote regions, resulting in a resurgence of malaria and polio.

Managua. Cardinal Miguel Obando y Bravo hears the confession of a parishioner.

Managua. Textile factory.

Masaya. Thousands of army reservists march through town preparing to defend the country from invasion.

*Río San Juan Department. U.S. citizen Eugene Hasenfus is led away
by the Sandinista soldiers who shot down his Contra supply plane.*

In October, the downing of a C-123 aircraft, with the subsequent capture of cargo handler Eugene Hasenfus and the plane's complete flight logs, provided the Sandinistas with hard evidence of the extensive U.S.–funded Contra supply operation. Hasenfus, sentenced in November to 30 years in prison, was released on humanitarian grounds one month later by the Nicaraguan government.

Tipitapa. Eugene Hasenfus in prison after sentencing.

1987

Managua. U.S. Assistant Secretary of State for Inter-American Affairs Elliot Abrams during a satellite press conference beamed to the U.S. Embassy.

In a public ceremony in January 1987, President Daniel Ortega signed Nicaragua's new constitution, committing the country to political pluralism, a mixed economy and nonaligned foreign policy. The document created the legal framework for revolutionary power, and the Sandinistas hoped it would help convince foreign and domestic critics that Nicaragua was a state of law. But the constitution was also a reaffirmation of longstanding Sandinista ideals and a source of national pride. Before the document was drafted, recommendations were sought from constitutional scholars worldwide, and about 100,000 citizens attended open meetings to make suggestions on its content.

In Washington, the Iran-Contra investigations were undermining the Reagan administration's authority and popularity, robbing the president of his power to induce Congress to approve more Contra aid. Yet Nicaragua's economic situation continued to worsen. Government workers had come to rely on a weekly bonus package of food and household goods that was sometimes more valuable than their wages. Prices rose so fast that the economy teetered on the edge of hyperinflation. For the first time in years, children could be seen begging or selling candy in the streets.

In addition, a fresh round of heavy fighting broke out, sparked by the previous year's $100 million in U.S. aid to the Contras. In August, when the five Central American presidents met in Guatemala to discuss peace, the Sandinistas were prepared to make significant concessions to end to the war. Costa Rica's President Oscar Arias arrived with a deal approved by Jim Wright, the Democratic Speaker of the U.S. House of Representatives. The proposal called for an immediate regional cease-fire; suspension of aid to all regional guerrilla movements; an amnesty for all rebels, followed by a dialogue with unarmed opponents; a ban on guerrilla use of territory in one state to attack another; democratization and free elections. The plan's acceptance by the Sandinistas shocked hardliners in the Reagan administration, who tried in vain to persuade their allies in Honduras and El Salvador to back out of the deal.

In October, President Arias won the Nobel Peace Prize for his efforts and was able to convince the Salvadoran and Honduran presidents to publicly urge the U.S. Congress not to approve any Contra-aid package. In response, the Sandinistas started to enact the provisions of the agreement: they lifted major portions of the state of emergency; they allowed *La Prensa* and Radio Catolica to reopen; they abolished the special courts set up to try security offenses; and they permitted opposition demonstrations. Most importantly, they set up a National Reconciliation Commission and invited their old enemy, Cardinal Obando y Bravo, to head it. Finally, in November, they agreed to indirect talks with the Contras mediated by Obando.

A key border crossing with Honduras was reopened for weekend family reunions. Thousands of Nicaraguans had fled to Honduras to escape the war or join the Contras, and joyful scenes of families reunited reinforced hopes for peace. But these hopes would not be easily realized.

Jinotega Department. A peasant woman crouches for cover as Sandinista troops come under fire.

Northern Jinotega Department. Contras with peasants.

Chontales Department. Contra troops.

*Chontales Department. Contra soldier plants a
land mine on one of the region's main roads.*

Abisinia, Jinotega Department. Members of a Miskito Indian family grieve for their father and husband, killed when Contras attacked the town earlier that day.

Quilalí. A woman readies a cross for the grave of her father, killed when he stepped on a Sandinista land mine.

In 1987, U.S. aid to the Contras reached its peak, resulting in the bloodiest year of the war. The Sandinista Defense Ministry estimated that an average of ten armed clashes occurred every day. Two major assaults—one along the Rama road in October, the other in December on the mining towns of Siuna, Rosita and Bonanza—made clear the Contras' ability to carry out large-scale attacks without prior detection by Sandinista intelligence.

Managua. Nicaraguan women celebrate Columbus Day at a U.S. Embassy party.

San Rafael del Norte. Town barber and coffin maker.

Managua. Sandinista party.

*Las Manos border station, Nicaraguan-Honduran border.
Family members embrace.*

On August 7, the Central American peace accord—also known as the Arias peace plan—was signed by the five Central American presidents in Esquipulas, Guatemala. In keeping with the spirit of the accord, Nicaragua and Honduras opened the Las Manos border crossing for weekend visits beginning in September. Tens of thousands of Nicaraguans traveled there to be reunited with family members who had fled to Honduras to escape the war or join the Contras.

Las Manos, Nicaraguan-Honduran border. Nicaraguan family reunites.

1988

Sapoá. *General Humberto Ortega receives signed peace accord from Contra leader Alfredo César as (left to right) President Daniel Ortega, Secretary General of the Organization of American States João Baena Soares, and Cardinal Miguel Obando y Bravo look on.*

Managua. First Communion.

Twice during the spring of 1988 the U.S. Congress rejected Reagan's latest Contra-aid request. The Arias peace plan and the Iran-Contra affair had finally taken their toll. In the meantime, the Sandinista army launched its biggest offensive ever, overwhelming the Contras and sending them reeling back to Honduras. The rebels were fast running out of funds and now realized that they, too, had good reason to discuss peace.

On March 23, grim-faced representatives of the two sides met for edgy talks at Sapoá, near the border with Costa Rica. They agreed to a 90-day cease-fire while negotiations proceeded. The talks raised hopes, but once again the White House was dismayed and encouraged the Contras to increase their demands to include the resignation of all Supreme Court justices and the rewriting of the constitution. The talks collapsed. Although the Contras were militarily spent and reduced to carrying out isolated ambushes and kidnappings in violation of the cease-fire, the specter of a U.S.–backed resumption of full-scale war enabled them to continue playing a vital political role in the U.S. effort to end Sandinista rule.

By now prices were out of control. High defense spending—41 percent of the national budget—pumped too much currency into circulation to spend on commodities made extraordinarily scarce by war and the trade embargo. By year's end, the annual inflation rate was 34,000 percent, and a trip to the market required a basketful of cash.

The anti-Sandinista opposition, spurred on by the U.S. Embassy, took advantage of the economic mayhem by encouraging strikes and demonstrations. One such march led to a pitched battle between baton-wielding police and stone-throwing youths. The government responded by expelling U.S. ambassador Richard Melton, and Reagan retaliated by expelling Carlos Tunnerman, Nicaragua's ambassador to both the U.S. and the Organization of American States. Speaker of the U.S. House of Representatives Jim Wright confirmed Sandinista accusations, saying, "We have received clear testimony from CIA people that they have deliberately done things to provoke an overreaction on the part of the government of Nicaragua." The CIA's tactics succeeded: the Sandinistas once again clamped down, jailing several opposition leaders. In response, Congress agreed to resume Contra funding, approving $75 million in so-called humanitarian aid. This enabled the rebels to buy everything except guns and bullets, which they still possessed in abundance.

The direct cost of the war, including material damage and lost harvests, was assessed at nearly $2 billion. Excess defense expenditures had cost another $2 billion, and lost income as a result of the U.S. trade and credit embargo amounted to a billion dollars more. The fighting had left 30,000 people dead; tens of thousands more wounded, kidnapped, or captured; and some 16,000 children orphaned. In October, just when it seemed as if nothing could get worse, the country was hit by Hurricane Joan. The Atlantic coast town of Bluefields was virtually flattened; the nationwide death toll was 148, and property damage was estimated at $840 million.

Jinotega Department. Sandinista soldiers celebrate the cease-fire accord signed March 23 at Sapoá.

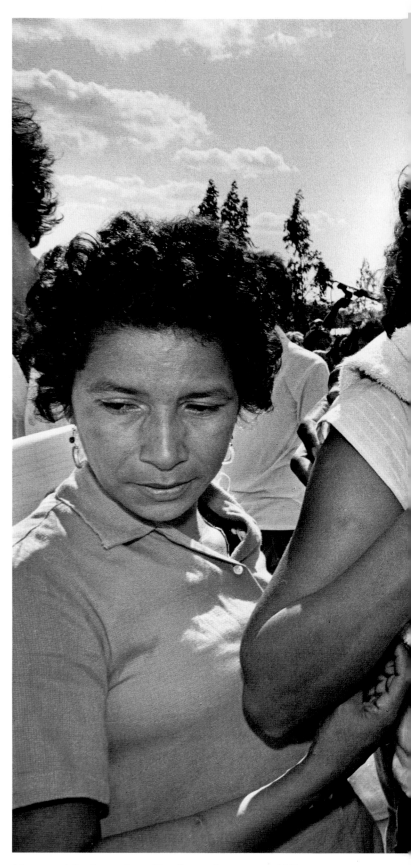

Managua. A family reunites with a former Contra, one of 100 prisoners released as part of the Sapoá peace agreement.

Yamales, Honduras. Early morning exercise at a Contra camp.

After having their military funding cut off by the U.S. Congress in February and being routed by Sandinista forces during "Operation Danto" in March, several thousand Contra soldiers and civilian supporters retreated to their Honduran base camps. Although strategicly defeated, the Contras received enough non-lethal aid from the United States to allow them to remain intact as an army, and to continue threatening Nicaraguan stability.

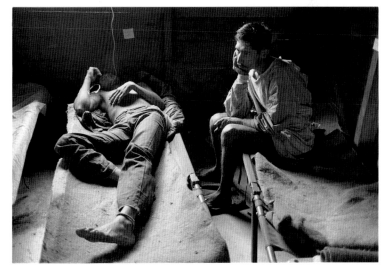

Yamales, Honduras. Contras in a field hospital.

Managua. Relatives of war victims demonstrate outside the offices of Cardinal Obando y Bravo, protesting his refusal to condemn Contra military activity.

Las Animas. Residents of the Monte Alto farm cooperative try to console a woman who has just learned of the death of her younger sister during a Contra attack on the co-op earlier that morning.

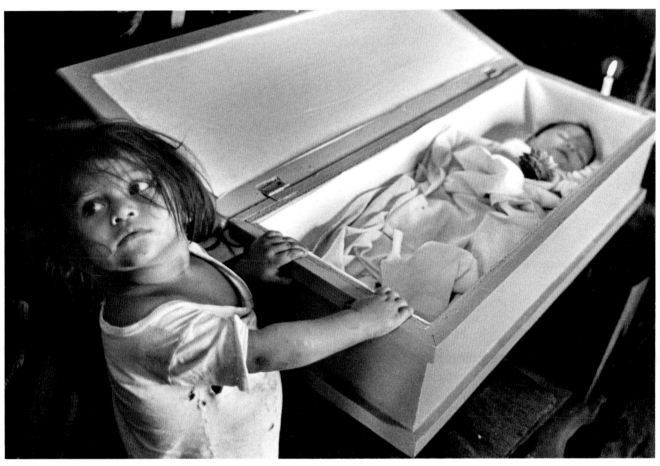

Jinotega Department. Wake for a six-month-old infant killed during a Contra attack on the Monterrey farm cooperative. The assault violated the Sapoá cease-fire, agreed upon five months earlier by Contras and Sandinistas.

Managua. Market vendor exchanges old bills for new currency issued by the government to combat rampant inflation.

Managua. Construction workers strike for increased wages as the inflation rate soars to 34,000 percent.

Managua. Sandinista police arrest striking construction worker.

Nandaime. Sandinista police break up opposition demonstration.

Nandaime. Sandinista police and opposition demonstrators clash.

Managua. Residents rummage through
garbage outside the city's Eastern Market.

*Managua. A mother holds her severely
dehydrated child in La Mascota hospital.*

1989

Managua. Nicaraguans say goodbye to loved ones as they begin their illegal journey to the United States.

At the end of 1988 and the beginning of 1989, thousands of Nicaraguans left the country fleeing poverty and the shattered economy. The majority traveled by bus to Guatemala, where they began an illegal and often dangerous journey through Mexico, before unlawfully crossing into the U.S.

*Managua. A soft-drink vendor passes a billboard reading
"Reagan is going! The revolution remains."*

"Reagan is going, but the policy remains the same," might well have been George Bush's slogan on inauguration day. The White House vowed continued support for the Contras, but Nicaragua's real headache was economic. Disposable income had dropped 90 percent in a decade, and export earnings now barely paid for a quarter of the nation's imports. Destruction of the economy had been the centerpiece of Reagan's strategy, designed to undermine Sandinista support and to be a warning to other countries not to copy Nicaragua's revolution.

In January, Ortega announced draconian austerity measures to curb inflation. These included firing or demobilizing 35,000 government workers and troops; slashing spending by 44 percent; pegging the national currency to the true market value of the dollar, causing massive devaluations; and allowing food prices to rise faster than wages. Ordinarily, Ortega's classic monetarist approach would have won bridging loans from the International Monetary Fund, but the U.S. persisted in vetoing such aid.

Throughout the decade, U.S. lobbying had effectively blocked Western loans, arms, oil, and machinery, forcing increased Sandinista reliance on Soviet-bloc support. So the sudden rapprochement between Moscow and Washington, and the collapse of the Warsaw Pact had a chilling effect. Not only were military and economic aid curtailed, but diplomatically the revolution was increasingly isolated. Moreover, as the elections approached, voters faced the prospect that the Soviets might no longer intercede to prevent economic collapse.

The only way to address the problem was to end the war. In February, the Central American presidents finally agreed to draft a plan to disarm the Contras, with the Sandinistas offering to move up elections and invite international observers. But the Bush administration refused to back the plan and struck a deal with the U.S. Congress to continue "humanitarian aid" to the Contras until February 1990.

The rebels began infiltrating back into Nicaragua, ambushing army patrols and stepping up their cease-fire violations. Nevertheless, the Sandinistas continued to meet the terms of the Arias plan. They forged an agreement with opposition political parties on conditions for the elections; released some 1900 ex-Guardia from jail; lifted the remaining provisions of the state of emergency; and held several days of voter registration that were praised by U.S. and other foreign observers.

On November 1, after Contras killed 23 people in ten days, Ortega announced an end to the cease-fire. Some feared the move was a Sandinista tactic to cancel the elections, but the campaign went ahead. Holding internationally supervised elections, with guaranteed media access for all parties, was a gamble, but the Sandinistas counted on the strength of their organization, the power of their rhetoric, and the memory of their early social and economic successes to carry the day. The opposition UNO was a ragtag alliance of 14 parties ranging from communists to hardline conservatives that united only at U.S. insistence. UNO was, the Sandinistas thought, too disorganized and too tainted by its wealthy conservative leadership to win an election.

Managua. A British volunteer trains a war-disabled veteran to repair wheelchairs at a cooperative workshop.

Thousands of foreign volunteers, known as internacionalistas, *came from more than 50 countries to work in medicine, construction, education, and agriculture.*

Jinotega Department. Coffee-picking brigade gathers in the early morning before their work day begins at the Monterrey farm cooperative.

*Masachapa. Woman wades to shore after greeting her
husband upon his return from a night's fishing.*

Rivas Department. Wedding day in Las Pilas.

Las Pilas. Grinding corn at the mill.

Diriamba. Performers reenact a centuries-old dance during the festival of San Vicente.

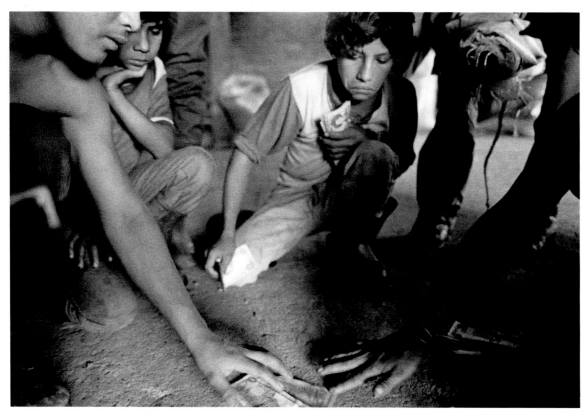

Jinotega Department. Local boys gamble their earnings from a day's work at the ENCAFE coffee warehouse at the Monterrey cooperative.

Jalapa. National Opposition Union (UNO) supporters on horseback
clash with Sandinista supporters in pre-election violence.

*Atlántico Norte. In the
isolated village of Wany,
campesinos register to vote.*

147

*Masatepe. UNO supporters ransack Sandinista campaign
offices at the end of a day of election violence.*

On December 10, supporters of the National Opposition Union (UNO) and the Sandinista Front clashed after an UNO campaign rally in Masatepe. One person was stabbed to death and more than 70 were injured during four hours of violence. It was the worst in a series of turbulent incidents surrounding the electoral campaign. There was concern from all quarters that continued conflict could jeopardize the electoral process. The Sandinista government moved swiftly to control the situation, increasing police presence and banning alcoholic consumption at campaign events. At the same time, Sandinista and UNO leaders called on their supporters to stay away from opponents' rallies. The moves were successful in virtually eliminating violence, and the elections continued without further incident.

Masatepe. A man injured at an UNO campaign rally.

1990

Jinotega Department.
Ballot in hand, an election
official explains the voting
procedure at a polling
place in a remote village.

On the night of Sunday, February 25, stunning results poured in from polling stations around the country. Desperate to end the war and revive the economy thousands of Sandinista supporters had joined opponents in voting for the victorious UNO candidate, Violeta Barrios de Chamorro.

Few had predicted such a result: not the FSLN, nor the CIA; not the UN observers, nor the U.S. media. In fact, the White House had made conciliatory statements in anticipation of a Sandinista victory. Even many UNO leaders were surprised by the election of Chamorro, the widow of Pedro Joaquín Chamorro, whose lifelong campaign against the Somozas had made him a national hero and whose assasination in 1978 had helped spark the revolutionary insurrection.

As the candidate backed by Washington and funded by millions of dollars from the U.S. National Endowment for Democracy, Chamorro's promises to secure U.S. financial backing and solve the economic crisis sounded convincing. She vowed to end the draft, and most Nicaraguans believed that her election would halt U.S. aid to the Contras and so finally stop the war. Her four children were evenly divided: two were committed Sandinistas and two fervent Contras. So when Chamorro spoke of national reconciliation, as she often did, her audience knew she meant it. While the newspaper she published, *La Prensa*, was regarded by many as a Contra mouthpiece, Chamorro herself had stayed aloof from party politics for ten years and had never directly endorsed the Contra war, allowing her to claim independence from what she described as the "warlike extremes."

Although Chamorro and the UNO coalition won the election, the Frente Sandinista received 41 percent of the vote, making it the single largest party in the country. The Sandinistas still controlled the army, police, judiciary, the largest trade unions, and enough seats in the National Assembly to require their approval for any constitutional changes. Ortega announced that the FSLN would respect the popular decision and transfer power. Nevertheless, the Frente committed itself to defending the revolution's major achievements, and in the two months before Chamorro's inauguration, used its majority in the outgoing National Assembly to pass legislation toward that goal. Furthermore, Ortega vowed, the Frente would continue to "govern from below."

On April 25, Inaguration Day, Ortega walked into the national baseball stadium in Managua. The bleachers were packed. Behind left field, a flood of red and black marked the Sandinista supporters; on the right, ranks of blue and white identified those of Chamorro. In a gesture of reconciliation, Ortega walked past the Chamorro partisans. He was chased away by a hail of stones and sticks. Minutes later Chamorro entered on the bed of a pickup truck. Dressed in white, arms outstretched, she was driven past the Sandinista supporters, but had to be protected by riot police from a hail of water bombs. After the two arrived at the ceremonial platform, Ortega removed his sash of office and placed it over Chamorro's shoulders. But as the ceremony itself demonstrated, after eight years of war and economic devastation, Nicaragua's wounds remained deep and its future far from certain.

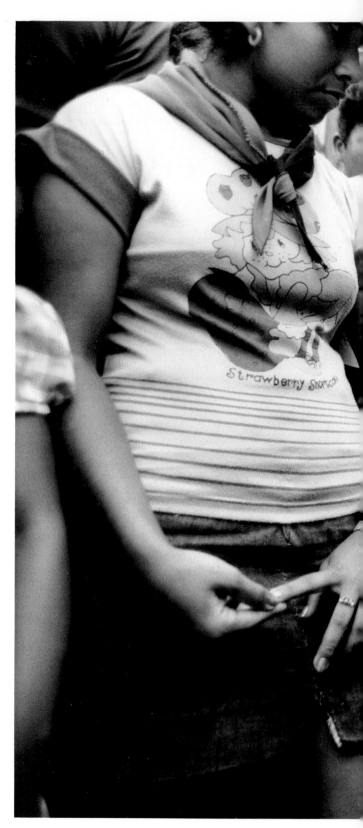

Puerto Cabezas. President Daniel Ortega greets supporters during a campaign rally.

Masatepe. Presidential candidate Violeta Chamorro campaigns amid supporters.

Niquinohomo. UNO supporters carry Chamorro aloft during a campaign rally.

Managua. UNO backers march to their final campaign rally.

Managua. Sandinista supporters await President Ortega.

*Jinotega. Campaign volunteer photographs President
Ortega with supporters and their children.*

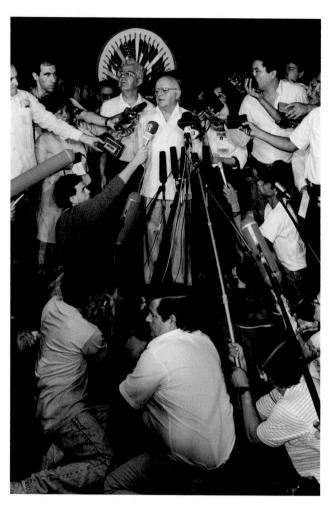

Managua. OAS Secretary General João Baena Soares holds a pre-election press conference. Thousands of of journalists and international observers converge on Nicaragua to monitor elections.

Masaya Department. Voting in El Comejón.

Managua. Violeta Chamorro, with vice-presidential candidate Virgilio
Godoy claims election victory, 4:00 a.m., February 26, 1990.

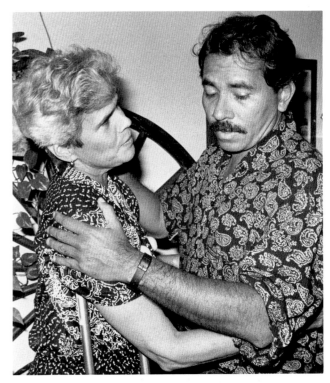

Managua. The day after the election, Daniel Ortega pays a congratulatory visit to Violeta Chamorro at her home.

EPILOGUE

In the aftermath of Violeta Chamorro's inauguration, the Sandinistas grappled with their new role as the country's main opposition force. Two FSLN-supported general strikes in the first three months of the new government made it clear that many Nicaraguans were willing to defend the revolution's reforms.

The Contras officially disbanded two months after Chamorro came to power, holding open the possibility of resurfacing as a political force. At the same time, the right wing of the UNO coalition began to criticize Chamorro, accusing her of accommodation with the Sandinistas; some UNO leaders talked openly of forming armed "National Salvation Brigades" to confront the FSLN.

While Nicaragua's future may be uncertain, the link with the past is clear: the revolution was born of genuine oppression and social injustice, and the FSLN will continue to receive significant support as long as those injustices remain.

Throughout the decade of revolution, Nicaraguans learned to participate in the political process and to demand social change, and in that sense have been permanently transformed. It may not be the only transformation the Sandinistas fought for, but this popular involvement in the political struggle guarantees that the final chapter in Nicaragua's odyssey toward national sovereignty and economic democracy has yet to be written.

"We feel pride in bringing to Nicaragua and to the people of Central America, to the people of Latin America and the Caribbean, to the people of the developing countries, in contributing—in this unjust world divided between the powerful and the weak—a little dignity, a little democracy, and a little social justice from this small territory in Central America, which saw the birth of men like Dario and Sandino, who made Nicaragua shine in the world."

—President Daniel Ortega Saavedra
from his message to the Nicaraguan people
6:00 a.m., February 26, 1990

CHRONOLOGY

Managua, 1979. Junta members after victory. (l-r) Alfonso Robelo; Moisés Hassan; Daniel Ortega; Violeta Chammorro; Sergio Ramírez.

1524 Spanish conquistadors defeat the Indians naming the newly conquered land "Nicaragua" after the Indian chief Nicarao.

1821 Central America declares its independence from Spain.

1855 North American adventurer William Walker invades Nicaragua, imposing slavery and declaring himself president. After a two-year rule, he is overthrown.

1909 The Liberal party government, led by José Santos Zelaya, refuses to grant interoceanic canal rights to the United States. The U.S. supports a successful revolt by the Conservative party.

1912 U.S. Marines land and begin 21 years of nearly continous occupation of Nicaragua.

1927 General Augusto César Sandino assembles an army of peasants and launches a guerrilla war against the U.S. occupation forces.

Rio San Juan, 1984. Former Sandinista hero Edén Pastora in the Nicaraguan jungle commanding his Contra army ARDE.

1933 Failing to defeat Sandino's guerrilla army, the Marines withdraw, after establishing the Nicaraguan National Guard with Anastasio "Tacho" Somoza García as its Commander-in-Chief.

1934 Sandino signs peace agreement with the new president, Juan Bautista Sacasa. On Somoza's orders, Sandino is assassinated on February 21.

1936 Somoza ousts Sacasa and takes the presidency.

1956 Somoza assassinated by poet Rigoberto López Pérez. The dictator's son Luís becomes president, and his second son, Anastasio, or "Tachito," takes over as Commander of the National Guard.

1961 Carlos Fonseca, Tomás Borge and Silvio Mayorga form the Sandinista National Liberation Front (FSLN). Two years later, the first guerrilla actions of the FSLN are taken near Río Bocay. Luís Somoza dies; his brother Anastasio Somoza succeeds him.

1972 Earthquake devastates Managua, killing 15,000. International relief aid is used to expand the Somoza family's business empire.

1974 FSLN stages an assault on a Somocista Christmas party, taking hostages. Somoza accedes to FSLN demands of ransom and prisoner releases.

1976 FSLN founder Carlos Fonseca is killed in combat with the National Guard. Tomás Borge is jailed in solitary confinement.

1977 The FSLN launches a major offensive throughout the country.

1978 Pedro Joaquín Chamorro, editor of *La Prensa* newspaper and leading opposition figure, is assassinated. FSLN commando seizes National Palace. FSLN-led insurrection takes the cities of Masaya, León, Chinandega, and Estelí for several days.

1979 **April**—The FSLN launches the "final offensive." **July**—Somoza resigns and flies to Miami. On July 19, Sandinista troops converge on the capital, ending the war against the Somoza dictatorship. The following day, 250,000 Nicaraguans celebrate in Managua's central plaza.

1980 **March**—The new government launches a massive literacy campaign, reducing the illiteracy rate from over 50% to 13%. **May**—U.S. Congress approves Carter administration request of $75 million economic aid package for Nicaragua.

1981 **January**—Ronald Reagan is inaugurated U.S. president. **March**— CIA forms Contra army from the remnants of Somoza's National Guard.

Boaco, 1984. Opposition presidential candidate Arturo Cruz (center).

April—Reagan administration cuts off all aid to Nicaragua. **July**—Agrarian Reform Law declares unproductive land may be confiscated for state farms, cooperatives, or individual peasants. **November**—The Reagan administration authorizes $20 million to destabilize the Nicaraguan government.

1982 **January**—Increased Contra activity on the Atlantic coast leads the government to relocate Miskito Indian communities from the Río Coco further inland. 10,000 Miskitos flee to Honduras. **March**—Following Contra destruction of two key bridges in the North, the government declares a state of emergency. **November**—U.S. Congress approves $24 million in covert aid to Contra rebels.

1983 **January**—Contadora Group is formed by Venezuela, Colombia, Mexico, and Panama to seek a peaceful solution to the Central American conflicts. **February**—Over 5,000 U.S. and Honduran troops take part in the "Big Pine" military manuevers 10 miles from the Nicaraguan border; further exercises follow in August.

Managua, 1984. Sandinista leader commandante Dora María Téllez speaks with mothers of army combatants.

March—Pope Paul II visits Nicaragua.
June—U.S. Treasury Department announces official policy of opposing all multilateral loans to Nicaragua.

October—CIA-trained saboteurs attack Nicaragua's largest port, Corinto, and destroy precious oil reserves.

1984 **March**—Violating international law, CIA mines Nicaraguan ports.
September—Nicaragua unconditionally accepts Contadora peace plan. U.S. blocks acceptance by the other Central American nations.
November—Democratic elections held. FSLN's Daniel Ortega is elected president. Reagan denounces the vote as a sham.

Timal, 1985. Fidel Castro speaks as Sandinista leaders look on.

December—U.S. Congress passes Boland amendment banning financial support for Contra military activites. Oliver North's "Project Democracy" continues funneling White House support.

1985 **February**—Sandinistas implement economic stabilization plan.
May—Reagan declares trade embargo against Nicaragua. Sandinistas allow Miskito Indians to return to Río Coco.
June—U.S. Congress approves $27 million in "humanitarian aid" to the Contras.

1986 **May**—ARDE, the main Contra grouping on Nicargua's southern border, disintegrates.
June—Approval of a $100 million Contra aid package by the U.S. Congress, including military aid. Sandinistas shut down Radio Católica and the opposition daily newspaper, *La Prensa*. Two church officials critical of the government are expelled.
June—The International Court of Justice finds the U.S. guilty of violating Nicaraguan sovereignty through its covert war.
October—U.S. cargo plane on a Contra resupply mission shot down; U.S. mercenary Eugene Hasenfus captured.
November—Iran-Contra scandal breaks in Washington.

1987 **January**—New constitution signed by President Ortega.
August—Presidents of Costa Rica, El Salvador, Guatemala, Honduras and El Salvador sign the Arias peace accords against the wishes of Washington.
September—Nicaraguan National Assembly approves autonomy statute for the Atlantic Coast.

San José, Costa Rica, 1989. The Central American presidents at a Mass for peace. (l-r) José Azcona of Honduras; Alfredo Cristiani of El Salvador; Oscar Arias of Costa Rica; Vinicio Cerezo of Guatemala; Daniel Ortega of Nicaragua.

Managua, 1985. Sandinista national directorate. (l-r) Tomás Borge; Victor Tirado; Humberto Ortega; Henry Ruíz; Daniel Ortega; Jaime Wheelock; Bayardo Arce; Carlos Núñez; Luís Carrión.

September-December—Nicaragua enacts provisions of the Arias peace accords. *La Prensa* and Radio Católica are allowed to resume production. A unilateral cease-fire is declared.

1988 **February**—Economic reform measures decreed, spearheaded by a change in currency. In the wake of the Arias peace agreement, U.S. Congress votes against further Contras aid.
March—Nicaraguan government and Contra representatives meet at Sapoá, and agree to a provisional cease-fire. Subsequent negotiations break down due to excessive Contra demands and U.S. hostility to the agreement.
July—Nicaragua expels U.S. Ambassador Richard Melton and seven diplomatic staff members charging them with involvement in an internal destabilization conspiracy.
September—Congress approves $75 million in "humanitarian aid" for the Contras.
October—Hurricane Joan slams through Nicaragua leaving $840 million in damages. 1988's inflation rises above 30,000%.

Yamales, Honduras, 1988. Top Contra military commander Colonel Enrique Bermúdez speaks to his men at a base camp.

November—George Bush, ex-CIA director is elected U.S. president. Bush declares his continued support for the Contras.

1989 **February**—The Central American presidents meet and reach an agreement on Contra demobilization. Nicaragua announces 1990 elections to be held in February, detailing procedures which will guarantee fair elections.
March—Congress approves $50 million in non-lethal aid to keep the Contras intact.
August—Central American leaders agree to December deadline for Contra demobilization under international supervision by the United Nations and the Organization of American States.
September—The National Opposition Union (UNO) selects *La Prensa* publisher Violeta Chamorro as their presidential candidate. The U.S. Congress approves overt aid for the UNO campaign.
December—Contras ignore demobilization deadline.

1990 **February**—Violeta Chamorro wins presidential election with 55% of the vote.
April—Chamorro inaugurated president of Nicaragua.
June—Contras demobilize.

PHOTO CREDITS

Front cover	**Perry Kretz**/Stern
Back cover	**Chris Vail**
Page 14	**Perry Kretz**/Stern
Page 16	**Pedro Valtierra**
Pages 18, 19	**Susan Meiselas**/Magnum
Page 20	**Claudia Gordillo**
Page 22	**Margarita Montealegre**
Page 24	**Koen Wessing**/Hollandse Hoogte
Page 26	**Susan Meiselas**/Magnum
Page 27, right	**Kit Hedman**
Page 28, top	**Matthew Naythons**/Gamma-Liaison
Page 28, bottom	**Kit Hedman**
Page 29	**Don Bartletti**/Los Angeles Times
Page 30	**Koen Wessing**/Hollandse Hoogte
Page 32	**Cordelia Dilg**
Pages 34-37	**Jamey Stillings**
Page 38	**Cordelia Dilg**
Pages 40, 41	**Jamey Stillings**
Page 42	**Haroldo Horta**/Zeitenspiegel
Page 44	**Cordelia Dilg**
Page 46	**Claudia Gordillo**
Page 48, left	**Antonio Turok**
Page 49	**Mike Goldwater**/Network
Page 50	**Murry H. Sill**
Page 51	**Cordelia Dilg**
Page 52	**Claudia Gordillo**
Page 54	**Antonio Turok**
Pages 56, 57	**Mario Tapia**/Barricada
Pages 58, 59	**Leonardo Barreto**/Barricada
Pages 60-63	**Claudia Gordillo**
Page 64	**Antonio Turok**
Page 66, top	**James Nachtwey**/Magnum
Page 66, bottom	**Claudia Gordillo**
Page 67	**Antonio Turok**
Page 68	**Claudia Gordillo**
Page 70	**Marvin Collins**/Impact Visuals
Page 72	**Antonio Turok**
Page 74, left	**Leonardo Barreto**/Barricada
Page 75	**María José Alvarez**
Page 76	**Bill Gentile**/Newsweek
Page 77, top	**Marvin Collins**/Impact Visuals
Page 77, bottom	**Wendy Watriss**
Page 78	**Abbas**/Magnum
Page 80	**Wendy Watriss**
Page 82	**Susan Meiselas**/Magnum
Pages 84, 85	**Lou Dematteis**
Page 86	**Andrew Ritchie**
Page 87, top	**Paolo Bosio**
Page 87, bottom	**Larry Boyd**
Pages 88, 89	**Lou Dematteis**
Page 90	**Maria Morrison**
Page 92	**Antonio Turok**
Page 93	**Lou Dematteis**
Pages 94, 96	**Lou Dematteis**/Reuters-Bettmann
Page 98, top	**Lou Dematteis**/Reuters-Bettmann
Page 98, bottom	**Susan Meiselas**/Magnum
Page 99	**Lou Dematteis**/Reuters-Bettmann
Page 100	**Claudia Gordillo**
Page 102, left	**Michelle Frankfurter**
Page 103	**Antonio Turok**
Page 104	**Haroldo Horta**/Zeitenspiegel
Page 106	**Lou Dematteis**/Reuters-Bettmann
Page 107, right	**Susan Meiselas**/Magnum
Page 108	**Lou Dematteis**/Reuters-Bettmann
Page 110	**Andrew Selsky**/AP
Page 112, top	**Bill Gentile**/Newsweek
Page 112, bottom	**Arturo Robles**/JB Pictures
Page 113	**Arturo Robles**/JB Pictures
Pages 114, 115	**Chris Vail**
Page 116	**Diego Goldberg**/Sygma
Page 117, top	**Horaldo Horta**/Zeitenspiegel
Page 117, bottom	**Diego Goldberg**/Sygma
Page 118, left	**Sylvia Plachy**
Pages 119, 120	**Lou Dematteis**/Reuters-Bettmann
Page 122	**Maria Morrison**
Pages 124, 125	**Lou Dematteis**/Reuters-Bettmann
Pages 126, 127	**Susan Meiselas**/Magnum
Page 128	**Chris Vail**
Pages 129-132	**Lou Dematteis**/Reuters-Bettmann
Page 133, top	**Lou Dematteis**/Reuters-Bettmann
Page 133, bottom	**Paolo Bosio**/AFP
Page 134, 135	**Robert Gentile**/Picture Group
Page 136	**Lou Dematteis**/Reuters-Bettmann
Page 138	**Chris Vail**
Page 140, left	**Jenny Matthews**/Network
Page 141	**Jane Stader**
Page 142	**Maria Morrison**
Page 143	**Donna DeCesare**/Impact Visuals
Page 144, top	**Samuel Barreto**
Page 144, bottom	**Jane Stader**
Page 145	**Peter Northall**/AFP
Page 146	**Lou Dematteis**/Reuters-Bettmann
Pages 148, 149	**Bill Gentile**/Newsweek
Page 150	**Susan Meiselas**/Magnum
Page 152	**Jeff Perkell**/Impact Visuals
Page 154	**Larry Boyd**/Impact Visuals
Page 155, right	**Lou Dematteis**/Reuters-Bettmann
Page 156, top	**Teun Voeten**
Page 156, bottom	**Mark Ludak**/Impact Visuals
Page 157	**Chris Vail**
Page 158, left	**Santiago Lyon**/Reuters-Bettmann
Page 159	**Dayna Smith**/Washington Post
Page 160	**Vince Heptig**/Reuters
Page 161, right	**José Rojas**
Page 162	**Michelle Frankfurter**

We wish to thank the following for their assistance in the gathering of, or for the use of, material in this book:

Agence France-Presse, AP/Wide World Photos, Barricada, Bettmann Newsphotos, Black Star, Gamma-Liaison, Hollandse Hoogte, Impact Visuals, JB Pictures, Magnum Photos, Network, Newsweek, Picture Group, Reuters, Sipa, Stern and Sygma.

REPUBLICA DE NICARAGUA

HONDURAS

RIO COCO

Saupuka

Waspam

TASBA PRI

JINOTEGA

ATLANTICO
NORTE

Puerto Cabezas

Yamales

Jalapa

NUEVA
SEGOVIA

Murra

Las Manos

Ocotal

San José
de Bocay

Wany

Quilali

Abisinia

MADRIZ

Pantasma

Mulukuku

San Jose de Cusmapa

Condega

Yali

ESTELÍ

San Rafael
del Norte

Apanas

RIO GRANDE DE MATAGALPA

Jinotega

GOLFO DE
FONSECA

Estelí

Tumarin

La Trinidad

Matagalpa

CHINANDEGA

MATAGALPA

Chinandega

LEÓN

BOACO

Corinto

Boaco

León

LAGO DE
MANAGUA

Rama

Tipitapa

Juigalpa

Bluefields

Managua

MASAYA

Masaya

CHONTALES

MANAGUA

Granada

ATLANTICO
SUR

OCEANO
PACIFICO

San Marcos

Masatepe

Dirizamba

Niquinohomo

Jinotepe

GRANADA

Masachapa

Nandaime

LAGO DE NICARAGUA

Las Animas

CARAZO

OCEANO
ATLANTICO

RIVAS

RIO
SAN JUAN

Rivas

Las Pilas

Sapoa

San Carlos

RIO SAN JUAN

COSTA RICA

FLA

CUBA

MEXICO

JAMAICA

BELIZE

GUATEMALA

HONDURAS

EL SALVADOR

NICARAGUA

OCEANO ATLANTICO

COSTA
RICA

OCEANO PACIFICO

PANAMA

COLUMBIA

CREDITS

Design and Production Director
Stephanie Sherman

Editors
Bernard Ohanian
Diana Reiss-Končar

Translation of Galeano Essays
Marcelo Montealegre "First Day in Nicaragua / 1980"
Gregory Rabassa "In Defense of Nicaragua / 1986"
Asa Zatz "A Child Lost in the Storm / 1990"
Diana Reiss-Končar additional translation

Copy Editor
Marjorie Baer

Cover Design
Fuenteovejuna

Photo Research Assistant
Cynthia Carris

ACKNOWLEDGMENTS

During the year and a half spent in the making of this book, dozens of people contributed images and ideas that helped shape its form and content.

First and foremost, a very special thanks goes to Susan Meiselas, without whose guidance and support this book would not have been possible. Her contributions, ranging from conception and design to photo research and editing to assistance in securing a publisher, were essential to this work's publication.

Special thanks also to Dr. Matthew Naythons, Rick Smolan and the staff of RxMedia: Liz Faulkner, Peter Goggin and Kate Warne. Their encouragement and generous contribution of work space and technology were key to the completion of this project.

We would also like to thank the following people who all helped in the making of this book: Susan Bergholz, Lars Bildt, Rob Brouwer, Jessie Bunn, Daniel Caselli, Lucinda Covert, Carlos Fernando Chamorro, Sergio de Castro, Warner Dick, María Fonseca, Bill Gentile, Claudia Gordillo, Kit Hedman, Lutz Kliche, Tom and Jane Kelly, Jonathan Mulcare, Manuel Pinel, Rick Rocamora and Scott Wallace.

Finally, we offer sincere thanks to all the photographers who supported this project, including those who submitted work that we were not able to include in this book.

BIOGRAPHIES

Lou Dematteis and **Chris Vail**, both from the United States, lived and photographed in Nicaragua during the height of the U.S.–backed Contra war. During the five years they were there, they often collaborated in documenting the brutal conflict and its effects on Nicaraguan society.

Uruguayan–born **Eduardo Galeano** is one of Latin America's most distinguished writers. His works include *Open Veins of Latin America* (1971); *Days and Nights of Love and War* (1978); and the three-volume *Memory of Fire: "Genesis"* (1982), *"Faces and Masks"* (1984) and *"Century of the Wind"* (1987). His forthcoming book, *The Book of Embraces*, will be published in English by W. W. Norton in the spring of 1991.

Anthony Jenkins was the London *Guardian*'s senior correspondent for Central America and the Carribean for four years. He is the author of the book *Nicaragua and the United States: Years of Conflict*, and has written for numerous publications in the U.S. and Europe. He currently works in New York as a freelance writer.